MASS COMMUNICATION & SOCIETY

Volume 3, Number 4, 2000 • Fall

SPECIAL ISSUE:
Advertising and Consumer Culture

GUEST EDITORS' NOTE VICES
Matthew P. McAllister and Sharon R. Mazzarella
Advertising and Consumer Culture 347

ARTICLES
Inger L. Stole
Consumer Protection in Historical Perspective: The Five-Year Battle
Over Federal Regulation of Advertising, 1933 to 1938 351

Judi Puritz Cook
Consumer Culture and Television Home Shopping Programming:
An Examination of the Sales Discourse 373

Wendy Siuyi Wong
The Rise of Consumer Culture in a Chinese Society: A Reading
of Banking Television Commercials in Hong Kong During the 1970s 393

Matthew Soar
Encoding Advertisements: Ideology and Meaning in Advertising Production 415

SCHOLARLY MILESTONES ESSAY
Stuart Ewen
Memoirs of a Commodity Fetishist 439

BOOK REVIEW
Paul McMasters
Reviews Jeffery A. Smith's *War and Press Freedom: The Problem of
Prerogative Power* 453

MASS COMMUNICATION & SOCIETY DIVISION INFORMATION

Mass Communication & Society is published four times a year by Lawrence Erlbaum Associates, Inc., 10 Industrial Avenue, Mahwah, NJ 07430–2262. Subscriptions are available only on a calendar-year basis.

Printed subscriptions for Volume 3, 2000 are US $35 for individuals and $185 for institutions within the United States and Canada; US $65 for individuals and $215 for institutions outside the United States and Canada. Faculty members of the Mass Communication & Society Division of the Association for Education in Journalism and Mass Communication pay $21 (individuals only); student members of the Mass Communication & Society Division of the Association for Education in Journalism and Mass Communication pay $12 (individuals only). Address changes: AEJMC Division members send changes to AEJMC; all others to the Journal Subscription Department, Lawrence Erlbaum Associates, Inc., 10 Industrial Avenue, Mahwah, NJ 07430–2262. Address changes should include the mailing label or a facsimile. Claims for missing issues cannot be honored beyond 4 months after mailing date. Duplicate copies cannot be sent to replace issues not delivered due to failure to notify publisher of change of address.

Electronic: Full price print subscribers to Volume 3, 2000 are entitled to receive the electronic version free of charge. *Electronic only* subscriptions are available at a reduced subscription price. Please visit the LEA website at http://www.erlbaum.com for complete information.

This journal is abstracted and/or indexed in *ComAbstracts, ComIndex,* and *Sociological Abstracts.*

Microform copies of this journal are available through Bell & Howell Information and Learning, P.O. Box 1346, Ann Arbor, MI 48106–1346.

Visit LEA's website at http://www.erlbaum.com and *Mass Communication & Society*'s website at www.wsu.edu/~mcs

MASS COMMUNICATION & SOCIETY, 2000, 3(4), 347–350

GUEST EDITORS' NOTE

Advertising and Consumer Culture

Matthew P. McAllister
Department of Communication Studies
Virginia Tech

Sharon R. Mazzarella
Department of Television–Radio
Ithaca College

The 1999 Fiesta Bowl was a proud moment in the history of University of Tennessee football. Beating Florida State University, the Vols won their second national championship in school history and the first for their coach, Phillip Fulmer. Perhaps the most glorious moment was to be the awarding of the national championship trophy on ABC television immediately after the game ended. However, as Coach Fulmer and his family and friends hugged each other on the award dais at the beginning of the presentation, a vice president from Tostitos, the sponsor of the bowl, shoved a bag of chips at the coach and asked, "how about a little bag of Tostitos, there?" At that moment, in front of millions, selling took precedent over sentiment.

It is no secret that we live in an advertising-oriented and consumer-based culture, as this story shows. Economically, for example, advertising is a massive institution. In 1998, for the first time in human history, one country—the United States—saw businesses spending more than $200 billion to advertise to its citizens (Coen, 1999). In the same year, one company, Procter & Gamble, spent more than $3 billion to advertise outside the United States, solidifying its global reach (Wentz, 1999). Culturally, advertising is a major symbol system in its own right, exposing us to thousands of promotional messages each week. These messages may bom-

Requests for reprints should be sent to Matthew P. McAllister, Department of Communication Studies, Virginia Tech, Blacksburg, VA 24061–0311. E-mail: mattm@vt.edu

bard us with social stereotypes (Kilbourne, 1999) or fragment us into niche-designed target markets (Turow, 1997). Institutionally, scholars have written about the increased influence of advertising and consumerism on such institutions as broadcasting generally (Andersen, 1995; Budd, Craig, & Steinman, 1999), public broadcasting specifically (Ledbetter, 1997), schools (Molnar, 1996), and children's entertainment (Pecora, 1998).

This special issue of *Mass Communication & Society* on advertising and consumer culture proposes to further the dialogue about the growing power of commercialization and consumerism. The authors of the four articles in this issue approach this topic from a variety of perspectives and methodologies.

The first article, by Inger Stole, is a meticulously researched accounting of the early battles waged over advertising regulation. Using archival research, Stole shows how legislation originally designed to protect consumers was, as a result of massive advertising industry lobbying, transformed into legislation that functioned more to protect advertisers. The ramifications of this early legislation, according to Stole, can still be seen today in the advertising industry's rampant use of puffery and promises of emotional and social rewards that products cannot really deliver.

One type of social reward often promised by advertising is class or status mobility—the promise that, by using a product, a person will appear to be of a higher social class than he or she really is. In her article, Judi Puritz Cook examines the phenomenon of home shopping channels to determine how issues of social class are incorporated into their sales discourse and specifically the class-based promises they make to viewers. Analyzing 2 weeks of programming on the home shopping channels, Home Shopping Network, Quality–Value–Convenience, and Q2, Cook shows how "the promise of status mobility through consumption" (p. 373) permeates the sales discourse of these channels—in particular the first two, which, she notes, are designed to appeal to a working-class audience and to encourage them to buy, buy, buy.

Although the United States has had many decades to become a consumer society, other countries are still fairly new to the process. Through her analysis of banking commercials in Hong Kong, Wendy Siuyi Wong shows how, since the 1970s, the discourse of these ads changed from a celebration of traditional Chinese values (including an emphasis on saving and hard work) to a celebration of more Western, consumer values (including the importance of spending and attaining material possessions). Supported by her in-depth analysis of sample commercials from two different Hong Kong banks, Wong suggests "that the process of modernization in Hong Kong was a process of Westernization, through which values and ideals developed in the West were imported to carry out the imperatives of consumer capitalism" (p. 412).

Finally, Matt Soar's article focuses on a subject all too often missing from studies of advertising and consumer culture—the advertising creatives themselves. Although advertising scholarship typically focuses on decoding messages, Soar's study, based on interviews with nine advertising professionals, is an analysis of the process of encoding such messages. Through these interviews, he finds that creatives' definition of successful advertisements is based less on sales effectiveness and more on creativity as it is defined by their peers in the industry. Modifying Richard Johnson's circuit of culture, Soar concludes that "in terms of cultural production [the creatives'] first audience, and hence their first source of inspiration, is themselves and their work" (p. 433).

As the contributor of the Scholarly Milestone Essay, we are honored to have Stuart Ewen, Professor and Chairman of the Department of Film and Media Studies at Hunter College and Professor in the PhD programs in History, Sociology, and American Studies at the Graduate Center of the City University of New York. Ewen's work pioneered critical approaches to advertising and consumer culture. His 1976 book, *Captains of Consciousness: Advertising and the Social Roots of Consumer Culture,* focused a critical eye on the development of advertising and greatly influenced later histories of advertising and media as well as research about the social influence of modern advertising. Highly praised by scholarly, trade, and popular publications when it was first published, this book has been cited by well over 300 academic journal articles. In 2001, a 25th anniversary edition with a new preface and illustrations will be published.

Ewen's later works on consumer and promotional culture have also been highly influential and lauded. *Channels of Desire: Mass Images and the Shaping of American Consciousness,* coauthored with Elizabeth Ewen and published in 1982, is still in print and it addressed the social issues involved with the mass production of messages. His 1986 book, *All Consuming Images: The Politics of Style in Contemporary Culture,* was a central source for Bill Moyers's 1989 PBS series, "The Public Mind." Ewen's (1996) latest book, *PR! A Social History of Spin,* was called by a reviewer in *The New York Times* (Newman, 1997) an "exhaustive and ambitious study" (p. G19); it chronicles the development of public relations and publicity in influencing public wants and undermining rational thought. Who better, then, to contribute the Scholarly Milestone Essay on advertising and consumer culture to this special issue?

Of course, the authors are but a few of the people responsible for this issue of *Mass Communication & Society.* We wish to thank the editor of the journal, David Demers, for giving us the opportunity to focus on this topic. We also owe a debt of gratitude to the many reviewers who worked hard—and on deadline—to provide valuable input to the articles submitted for this special issue. These reviewers were Amy Aidman, Robin Andersen, Jane Banks, Susan B. Barnes, Mary Bentley, Bonnie S. Brennen, Duncan H. Brown, Raymond Gozzi, Rachel L. Holloway, W. Wat Hopkins, Gina Marchetti, Norma Pecora, Mary Beth Oliver, Edward H. Sewell, Jr., Jane Stokes, Lance Strate, Jill Swenson, Jonathan Tankel, Joseph Turow, Angharad Valdivia, Christopher A. Vaughan, and Karin G. Wilkins.

REFERENCES

Andersen, R. (1995). *Consumer culture and TV programming.* Boulder, CO: Westview.

Budd, M., Craig, S., & Steinman, C. (1999). *Consuming environments: Television and commercial culture.* New Brunswick, NJ: Rutgers University Press.

Coen, R. J. (1999, May 17). U.S. ad growth hits 7.5% in '98 to outpace GDP. *Advertising Age,* p. 30.

Ewen, S. (1976). *Captains of consciousness: Advertising and the social roots of the consumer culture.* New York: McGraw-Hill.

Ewen, S. (1986). *All consuming images: The politics of style in contemporary culture.* New York: Basic.

Ewen, S. (1996). *PR! A social history of spin.* New York: Basic.

Ewen, S., & Ewen, E. (1982). *Channels of desire: Mass images and the shaping of American consciousness.* New York: McGraw-Hill.

Kilbourne, J. (1999). *Deadly persuasion: Why women and girls must fight the addictive power of advertising.* New York: Free Press.

Ledbetter, J. (1997). *Made possible by ... : The death of public broadcasting in the United States.* New York: Verso.

Molnar, A. (1996). *Giving kids the business: The commercialization of American schools.* Boulder, CO: Westview.

Newman, J. (1997, March 2). Books in brief: Nonfiction. *The New York Times,* p. G19.

Pecora, N. O. (1998). *The business of children's entertainment.* New York: Guilford.

Turow, J. (1997). *Breaking up America: Advertisers and the new media world.* Chicago: University of Chicago Press.

Wentz, L. (1999, November 8). P&G tops $3 bil mark in non-US ad spending. *Advertising Age,* p. 12.

MASS COMMUNICATION & SOCIETY, 2000, 3(4), 351–372

Consumer Protection in Historical Perspective: The Five-Year Battle Over Federal Regulation of Advertising, 1933 to 1938

Inger L. Stole

Department of Advertising
University of Illinois at Urbana–Champaign

The 5-year period between 1933 and 1938 represents a critical juncture in the history of advertising. It was during this period, and only during this period, that Congress formally considered exactly what should be the role of advertising in our society and how it should be regulated. In this article, I chronicle some of the main issues and developments behind the struggle over the crafting and passing of legislation for the regulation of advertising that took place in the 1930s. I discuss how the Tugwell bill (S. 1944, 1934), a radical measure drafted with consumer protection in mind, evolved into the Wheeler–Lea Act of 1938, a law that rendered such protection virtually painless from advertisers' perspective. Noting that the Wheeler–Lea Act, after more than 6 decades, is still the major law on advertising regulation, the article points to some of its modern implications and evaluates its current value.

(Advertising commands a large presence in our society) Over $200 billion was spent on advertising in the United States in 1998, and the 1999 figure was approximately $212 billion (Beatty, 1998; Coen, 1999; Elliot, 1998). Advertising accounts for more than 2% of the U.S. gross domestic product, making it one of the largest industries in the economy. In view of this extensive commercial education, one may expect that U.S. consumers would possess, or at least have access to, a great deal of information about the various goods and services in the marketplace. The paradox of advertising is that this, in fact, is not the case. Perhaps it is an exaggeration, but

---

Requests for reprints should be sent to Inger L. Stole, Department of Advertising, University of Illinois at Urbana–Champaign, 103 Gregory Hall, 801 South Wright Street, Urbana, IL 61801. E-mail: istole@uiuc.edu

one could almost argue that the more a person is exposed to advertising, the less capacity he or she has to make an informed decision in the marketplace. At any rate, there is little evidence that massive exposure to advertising produces more informed and prudent consumers. This should not be a surprise. In place of price and product information, advertisers tend to promise sex, romance, beauty, popularity, or some other ephemeral result in exchange for brand loyalty. Most claim to have the best, most dependable, and best valued product on the market, but few care to substantiate these claims. What is striking about the lion's share of advertising is the lack of reliable and trustworthy price and product information (Christians, Fackler, Rotzoll, & McKee, 1997; Jacobson & Mazur, 1995; Savan, 1994).

The U.S. government, through the Federal Trade Commission (FTC), is authorized to regulate advertising on behalf of the public. In theory, the FTC's job is to see that advertising does not deceive the public and that it provides a positive service. The law that authorized this regulation, the Wheeler–Lea Act, commonly known as the Wheeler–Lea amendments, to the Federal Trade Commission Act, was passed by Congress and signed into law in 1938. As it was passed at the height of the New Deal with the blessing of the Roosevelt Administration, it is easy to regard the Wheeler–Lea amendments as some sort of proconsumer, antibusiness initiative, and there is an element of truth to that perspective. However, the FTC regulation authorized by the Wheeler–Lea amendments has made dubious advertising practices perfectly legal. Manufacturers are free to promise the most outrageous emotional awards in exchange for brand loyalty. Even if drinking a particular brand of coffee fails to represent "the best part of waking up" or the skies of United Airlines prove to be unfriendly, advertisers have only expressed their own evaluations of their products; this, according to the law, represents trade puffery, not explicit falsehood, which the Wheeler–Lea amendments directly forbid (Preston, 1996). It is ironic that the very law that supports advertisers in their use of hype and puffery came into existence as the result of a movement intent on altering such practices.

The 5-year period between 1933 and 1938 represents a critical juncture in the history of U.S. advertising, for it was during this period, and only during this period, that Congress formally considered exactly what the role of advertising should be in our society and how it should be regulated. The purpose of this article is to chronicle some of the main issues and developments in the 5-year struggle that took place in the 1930s to craft and pass legislation for the regulation of advertising and to show why the eventual Wheeler–Lea amendments differed so drastically from the original intent of the 1930s advertising regulation sponsors and advocates. In his work on broadcasting in the 1930s, McChesney (1993) observed that the legislative deliberations surrounding radio regulation in the 1930s were dominated by powerful business interests and that the public was largely ignorant of and uninvolved in the policy-making process. The debate over advertising regulation during the same period followed the same pattern. Given the uneven playing field, it should be no surprise that the regulation of advertising authorized by the Wheeler–Lea amendments complemented the goals and needs of the advertising industry while proving largely ineffectual from the standpoint of consumers.

Given that the law has just entered its seventh decade as the major law regulating U.S. advertising, it is striking that only two scholars have written in any detail on the development and passage of the Wheeler–Lea amendments. (By comparison, scholarly books, dissertations, and articles on the history of legislation for broadcast regulation would fill many library bookshelves.) Pease (1958), who provided a solid general overview, and Tedlow (1981), who examined the legal implications of the Wheeler–Lea amendments, provide the best accounts of the law to date. This article complements Pease's and Tedlow's findings while providing two perspectives insufficiently present in Pease's and Tedlow's fine works. First, I attempt to put advertising and advertising regulation in more of a historical and political economic context. Second, I emphasize the importance of the consumer movement and public discontent with advertising as factors that drove much of the political momentum to pass legislation for the regulation of advertising. Moreover, I employ numerous archival sources that were unavailable to either Pease or Tedlow and that, in my view, highlight the importance of these two factors in explaining the process by which the Wheeler–Lea Act was drafted and passed into law. In sum, this article locates the 1930s demand for advertising regulation as a response to new marketing practices. Rather than providing consumers with facts and information, firms operating in oligopolistic markets focused on brand loyalty in their advertising. In many categories, there were hardly any competitive differences between the various products. Consumers were asked to choose a product based on the image that advertisers had created around it. Whereas this practice—commonly referred to as parity advertising—quickly evolved into a major marketing tool for business, consumer advocates were less impressed. By the early 1930s, they demanded that Congress pass legislation to protect consumers from this marketing practice. From the state of present-day advertising, it is evident that this crusade largely failed. I endeavor to explain in this article why this took place and why the Wheeler–Lea Act, instead of providing stronger consumer protection, ended up protecting the very practices it sought to regulate.

DEMANDS FOR ADVERTISING REGULATION: THE ROAD TO THE TUGWELL BILL

The late 19th and early 20th centuries witnessed massive changes both in production and marketing of consumer goods. For example, from 1900 to 1930, when the population of the United States increased by 65%, manufacturers' volume increased by 151% (Harris & Milkis, 1989). The same period witnessed a rise in oligopolistic markets. These markets are dominated by a handful of large firms, each with a significant market share. Because members of each oligopolistic market tend to make very similar products, advertising serves to establish a brand identity around a given product or service. Advertising copy that appeals to consumers' sense of reason and provides information that enables them to comparison shop does not serve the manufacturer if no real differences exist between the dominant brands in the market. To tell the truth about a product—that it costs the same as its competition and is basically identical in quality—hardly developed brand loyalty or lured new users. Hence, a major trend in modern advertising was to employ puffery, imagery, and emotional or irrelevant claims in advertising messages (Baran & Sweezy, 1966; Curti, 1967; McAllister, 1996; Veblen, 1921/1938, 1923/1954).

The 1920s witnessed an increase in advertisements that magnified minor problems, to the point where they appeared crucial to important life decisions. Instead of providing consumers facts and information about the various products, advertisements tended to coach and guide them to goods with the "right" image (Marchand, 1985). In addition, there was considerable incentive for some advertisers to shade the truth, even to mislead or lie, if it would enhance product sales. It did not take long before such marketing strategies caught the attention of a feisty and burgeoning consumer movement.

This tension between the rapidly emerging institution of modern advertising and its opponents came to a head in the 1930s. A consumer movement had been building strength and momentum since the early years of the 20th century, but whereas the early consumer movement had focused on improvements in food sanitation and workers' conditions, the 1930s movement had shifted its primary concern to citizens' rights in a rapidly commercialized society. Rather than fighting advanced capitalism, the consumer movement wanted to make the system accountable to those it claimed to serve. Professional women's organizations like the General Federation of Women's Clubs, the American Home Economics Association, and the National League of Women's Voters and more radical groups like Consumers' Research and Consumers Union stressed people's right to receive adequate information about the goods they consumed. Recognizing advertising as the major, if not only, forum where manufacturers could explain their products to the public, the consumer movement sought to alter the manner in which ads addressed consumers. Rather than confuse and impress, argued consumer advocates, ads should provide potential consumers with more information about the various products. Before long, the consumer movement had made federal legislation of advertising one of its key issues ("Food and Drugs," 1933; Kallet & Schlink, 1933; Schlink, 1933a).

That no federal regulation of advertising was on the books before the 1900s is a sign that advertising is a relatively recent phenomenon. The first halting move to address the problems of the new era came in the 1906 Food and Drug law that made misbranding foods and drugs illegal. However, the law made no mention of advertising; it applied only to labeling and manufacturing goods (Lynd, 1934). Adding to consumer advocates' dismay was the fact that the FTC, which had been established in 1914, held the power only to regulate advertising if and when it caused one business to hold an unfair advantage over another. The commission could not interfere on consumers' behalf. In view of the repeated scandals with fraudulent advertising and the public dissatisfaction with misleading advertising as reflected in the growth of the consumer movement, it was an untenable situation (Scientific Consumer Purchasing, 1934–1935; Tedlow, 1981; Thompson, 1938a).

By the time of Franklin D. Roosevelt's inauguration in March 1933, considerable momentum existed on behalf of establishing formal federal regulation of advertising. In June of that year, Senator Royal S. Copeland (Dem., NY) introduced a bill to amend and revise the existing Food and Drug Act (Young, 1967/1992). The bill, which had been drafted under the supervision of the Food and Drug Administration (FDA), won strong endorsements from the Assistant Secretary of Agriculture, Rexford G. Tugwell, and it was soon referred to as the Tugwell bill (S. 1944, 1934). Not only did the proposed law suggest new labeling laws and mandatory grading of goods, it also sought to empower the FDA to prohibit false advertising of any food, drug, or cosmetic. A false ad was defined as one that created a misleading impression by the use of "ambiguity or inference" (Pease, 1958; Young, 1967/1992). Advertisements were defined as representations of fact or opinion disseminated in any manner or by any means other than by labeling.

THE ADVERTISING INDUSTRY REACTS
TO THE TUGWELL BILL

The pending legislation did not take the advertising industry—meaning the trade associations representing national advertisers, advertising agencies, and commercial media—by surprise. The public's concern over false and misleading advertising had caused industry worries for quite some time. This was reflected in the many self-regulatory attempts, some going as far back as the 1910s. Unfortunately for the industry, however, most of its self-regulation failed due to lack of enforcement (Pease, 1958; Stole, 1998). On realizing that its tries at self-regulation had proven ineffective in preventing a measure like the Tugwell bill from being introduced, industry leaders were at least determined to render the legislation as mild on advertising as possible.

Recognizing the value of organized opposition, the advertising industry launched a massive attempt to undermine the proposed legislation ("Why All Advertisers," 1933). Although different groups within the larger advertising community had their own, quite specific objections to the Tugwell bill, most objected to the bill's criteria for determining misleading advertising claims. If written into law, the measure would make it close to impossible for manufacturers to infer ambiguous rewards such as popularity, marital happiness, and social acceptance in exchange for product loyalty. The bill held the potential to throw the entire consumer economy for a loop. "Large publishing, advertising and broadcasting interests have been demanding a clean-up of shady advertising habits," observed *Business Week* ("Advertising or Tugwell," 1933, p. 14) in a very apt summary of the advertising industry's reactions to the proposed law. "But they became somewhat breathless after a look inside the mouth of the Tugwell bill. They wanted a measure with teeth in, but nobody expected a crocodile" (p. 14).

Advertisers feared that if the Tugwell bill became law, advertising puffery would be prohibited as false and misleading. The president of the American Association of Advertising Agencies (AAAA) John Benson (*Food, Drugs, and Cosmetics Hearings,* 1934b) was particularly upset. He argued that there was no way advertising could be restricted to a "cold statement of facts" (p. 331). Advertising, according to Benson, was a special plea. It was "salesmanship in print" (p. 331) and could not be subjected to a juridical analysis. Congressional supporters did not deny that *ambiguity* and *inference* were rather vague terms but argued that they were important to secure a flexible law that could stop a wide variety of violations ("Nine Objections," 1933).

The Tugwell bill met some of its stiffest resistance from the Proprietary Association, which argued that the bill's criteria was so strict that only 10% of advertising would be able to meet the proofs it set forth ("Ambiguity of Tugwell Bill," 1933; "Drug Act Revision," 1933; *Food, Drugs, and Cosmetics Hearings,* 1934a; "Proprietary Association," 1933; Rorty, 1934/1976; "Tug-O-War," 1933; "Tugwell Bill Is Target," 1933).

From the standpoint of the advertising industry, the consumer movement and its legislative demands could hardly have arrived at a more inopportune time. The industry, like most other businesses, had been devastated by the Great Depression. By 1933, the amount spent for advertising had plummeted more than 50% from its 1929 level of $2 billion ("Advertising—Brief Survey," 1939; Fox, 1984/1997; Hodges, 1934). Mass media were severely affected. From the 1929 total as a base, newspaper advertising, for example, dropped 15% in 1930, 24% in 1931, 40% in 1932, and touched bottom with a 45% dip in 1933 (Mott, 1962, p. 675). In an effort to win support against the Tugwell bill, advertisers and their agencies flooded newspapers, radio, and magazines with letters and analyses that predicted even larger revenue losses should the bill slip through Congress. The majority of mass media outlets succumbed to the advertising industry's pressures by omitting coverage of the pending legislation, thus keeping the issue off the public's news agenda ("Advertising Censorship," 1933; *Food, Drugs, and Cosmetics Hearings,* 1934c, 1934e; Hedges, 1933; "Last Roundup," 1933; "Publishers of Evening Tribune," 1933; Witherspoon, 1998). Bill opponents were equipped with sizable war chests for public relations campaigns and lobbying efforts. Powerful drug interests, constituting one of the largest groups of advertisers, were the strongest opponents of the proposed legislation (Witherspoon, 1998). In 1934, they formed the Joint Committee for Sound and Democratic Consumer Legislation, with the specific goal of fighting the Tugwell bill (The Joint Committee For Sound and Democratic Consumer Legislation, n.d.).

Bill supporters, on the other hand, had far fewer funds and resources. Tugwell and the officials of the FDA had to rely on the support of a handful of liberal and radical publications that carried little or no advertising, on the desultory and disorganized support of the medical profession, and on the intermittent and poorly financed help of a few women's and consumer organizations ("Last Roundup," 1933; Rorty, 1934/1976). The financial resources and command of the advertising industry over the commercially sponsored mass media industries greatly concerned consumer advocates. Frederick Schlink (1933), the leader of Consumers' Research, was worried.

> The manufacturers are fully informed through their trade press and through private channels of information, lobbyists in Washington, lawyers etc. what is going on and what general direction it is likely to take. Consumers [on the other hand] are practically not being reached with respect to the intended changes because the newspapers and popular magazines ignore the story or play it down. (p. 1)

In the interest of consumers, Schlink urged the government to sponsor a campaign informing people about the bill and its merits. Unfortunately for Tugwell bill supporters, the FDA had no propaganda budget, although it did manage to stage an exhibit at the 1933 World's Fair that was later shown, on request, to women's clubs and other organizations. This modest attempt was greeted with howls of protest from the patent medicine lobby (Rorty, 1934/1976). The Joint Committee on Sound and Democratic Consumer Legislation was outraged, for example, when supporters of the Tugwell bill were given time to present their views over the National Broadcasting Corporation (NBC) Red Network (Jacobs, 1933).

During the preparatory stages of the bill, Consumers' Research had willingly shared research obtained in connection with *100,000,000 Guinea Pigs* (Kallet & Schlink, 1933), a hugely successful consumer advocacy book, with Tugwell and his colleagues in the Department of Agriculture. However, working as the extended arm of the government soon became a financial strain on the organization (Kallet & Schlink, 1933; Schlink, 1933a). Preparation of the new law, stated Consumers' Research, was better left to the government, which had far more resources at its command. The organization recognized that intense propaganda activity in connection with the Tugwell bill would come to disrupt its normal functioning completely and make it impossible for Consumers' Research to continue the regular output of publications on which the public had come to expect (Kallet, 1934a). Although limited funds prevented the organization from matching the lobbying strategies of its opponents in the advertising community, Consumers' Research still tried to get its opinions across. This was not always easy. Arthur Kallet's (1934b) attempts to have the group's viewpoints represented at the various Congressional hearings over the Tugwell bill and its many successors illustrates this point quite clearly.

1933–1934 HEARINGS ON S. 1944
AND ITS SUCCESSORS

The first hearings on S. 1944 were held in early December 1933. Drug and cosmetics manufacturers were most strongly opposed to the bill and demanded it be killed, while other interested parties, such as newspapers, magazines, and the majority of the advertising community, desired substantial revisions ("N.P.A. 'Tugwell Committee,'" 1933; "Tugwell Bill Center," 1933). The bill enjoyed its strongest support among mainstream consumer organizations, particularly women's clubs. The American Medical Association (AMA), *The Nation*, *The New Republic*, *Good Housekeeping*, and to a certain degree *Advertising and Selling* also endorsed the measure (Pease, 1958; "Last Roundup," 1933). The radical wing of the consumer movement, on the other hand, believed that the bill did not provide enough in terms of consumer protection and wanted S. 1944 passed only if there were no hope for a stronger law (*Food, Drugs, and Cosmetics Hearings*, 1934d).

Senator Copeland, who had introduced the bill in the Senate, presided over the hearings. Copeland was an avowed and sincere conservative who frequently opposed President Roosevelt and the New Deal, and many found it rather curious that the senator was asked to introduce a measure calling for radical government regulation of business. This contradiction did not escape the attention of Kallet (*Food, Drugs, and Cosmetics Hearings*, 1934d) of Consumers' Research, who accused Copeland of siding with the opponents of the bill. Kallet lambasted the senator for not allowing consumer interests enough time to explain their concerns over the bill while devoting ample time to complaints from commercial interests. He also questioned Copeland's integrity by suggesting that consumers could not receive fair play from a person who received pay for broadcasts on behalf of a product that, under the terms of the pending legislation, would be adversely affected as having been untrue or misleading. Kallet was referring to Copeland's broadcasts on behalf of Fleischmann's Yeast ("Drug and Yeast," 1933) started after the introduction of the pending bill. On behalf of Consumers' Research, Kallet went as far as demanding the hearings be reconvened under a new committee and an impartial chairman.

Most members of the advertising community detected no trace of a business conspiracy. Quite to the contrary, they viewed the bill as yet another expression of New Deal business hostility ("Is U.S. Against," 1933). This was an overly sensitive reaction, however. Although President Roosevelt quite clearly favored some form of advertising regulation, he was by no means against advertising per se and was less in favor of strict advertising regulations than critics gave him credit for. This became increasingly evident as Roosevelt showed a rather noncommittal attitude toward S. 1944 ("Advertising and the U.S.," 1933; "Backs Food," 1933).

By late 1933, it had become quite evident that S. 1944 would not be passed into law. The combined advertising community lobbied vigorously against the measure, and consumer advocates, holding out for a bill with more consumer protection and the President's support, were not eager to see it passed either ("Is the Tugwell Bill," 1933). The first revision changed the bill's criteria for false and misleading advertising. Contrary to S. 1944, S. 2000 (1934) left no room for consumers' input in determining whether an advertisement should be deemed false through the use of ambiguity and inference. The new version demanded that "substantial medical opinion or demonstrable scientific facts" be consulted before an ad met the criteria ("Drastic Revisions," 1934, p. 1). S. 2000 proposed to establish advisory health and food committees to aid the Department of Agriculture in determining what constituted false and misleading advertising. Advertisers were assured that these government-appointed committees would be staffed with several business-friendly individuals (*National Association of Broadcasters Reports*, 1934a, 1934b; Nichols, 1934; "Self Regulation," 1934).

The advertising community expressed relief. *Printers' Ink* ("Four Food Bills," 1934) reflected "It looked pretty bad three months ago, when the then Tugwell bill, being an Administration measure, seemed slated for inevitable enactment. But the moderates got in their work and we now have the Copeland bill" (p. 69). Consumers' Research (Kallet, 1934a), on the other hand, was outraged. "The bill is bad," argued Kallet, "largely because the politicians and the courts in which hands the protection of consumers would remain are willing servants of the business interests and have little genuine interest in the public welfare" (p. 1). A frustrated Tugwell (1934) reached his breaking point when President Roosevelt intervened and sided with Senator Copeland in a discussion over provisions in the original bill, which Tugwell wanted to keep intact but Senator Copeland wanted to change.

> Senator Copeland, after our conversation the other day, apparently thought he had a mandate from you to kill every provision of the bill which would be of any use, [a disgusted Tugwell wrote to President Roosevelt]. He has virtually allowed the people who have been making the personal attacks on me all summer to rewrite it to suit themselves; in fact, they wrote the language now incorporated in it. In view of everything, I am going to be compelled to announce my own withdrawal and to explain how Senator Copeland has handed our measure over to our opponents who would have been regulated under it. (p. 2)

Another round of minor changes resulted in S. 2800 (1934), a bill even more to the advertising community's liking. The new version offered no provisions for mandatory grading of goods. This was a victory for major food manufacturers, who had argued that such labeling represented an infringement on brand names and, as such, a direct competition to advertising. Major women's groups, including the American Home Economics Association, on the other hand, were very upset about changes introduced in S. 2800 ("Consumers in Limelight," 1934).

Printers' Ink ("Copeland Bill Slated," 1934) declared in the following:

> The Copeland bill as it now stands, is so vastly superior to the original Tugwell measure—a glaring monstrosity in the way of legislation, if there ever was one—that most advertisers will probably accept it with little further argument. (p. 21)

Consumers' Research, on the other hand, offered a new set of objections to the revised version. The organization maintained that S. 2800, with its emphasis on industry profits over consumer safety, did not even come close to providing the kind of protection consumers should demand (*Commerce,* 1934b). Advertising practitioner turned critic, James Rorty (*Commerce,* 1934c), concurred.

> I do not believe that Congress can or will fully protect and serve the public in this or any other bill, [he stated]. Why? The reason in my belief, is that adequate legislation cannot be passed in the face of tremendous opposition of the food, drug, cosmetic and advertising and publishing interests. (p. 410)

Kallet agreed. He was particularly upset over the fact that S. 2800 was intended as a retroactive measure against false and misleading advertising and not, as the original Tugwell bill had stipulated, a measure to prevent such forms of advertising from appearing in the first place. Frustration with the legislative developments caused Consumers' Research (*Commerce,* 1934b; "Six Bills," 1934) to write and introduce the Boland bill (H.R. 8316, 1937), a radical measure that went beyond the original Tugwell bill but never went anywhere on Capitol Hill. Kallet also charged that the Senate Commerce Committee under its chairman Hubert D. Stephens granted more time for business to be heard than consumer organizations. Only after sending a telegram of complaint to President Roosevelt and aggressively pressuring Senator Stephens for a chance to express the point of view of Consumers' Research was Kallet given the floor for 30 minutes (Kallet, 1934b).

EFFORTS TO DRAFT A SUCCESSOR
TO THE TUGWELL BILL

Over the next year a new—and for advertising interests, an increasingly lenient—version of the bill, S. 5 (1935), was prepared. A relieved Association of National Advertisers (ANA) noted that almost all major objection raised by advertisers in reaction to the original (S. 1944) bill had now been resolved. The definition of false advertising had been greatly simplified and made easier on advertisers, compulsory government grading and voluntary inspection service for factories at manufacturers' expense had been dropped, and the Secretary of Agriculture, who had been given huge discretionary powers under the Tugwell bill, was now replaced by advisory committees where advertisers had a say. S. 5 also spared manufacturers from disclosing their secret formulas and recipes and drastically reduced the number of palliative medicines required to carry the words "Not a Cure" in equal size and prominence with the name of the drug. Much to media owners' relief, the new version stated quite clearly that responsibility for false advertising rested with advertisers alone ("A.N.A. Withholds Approval," 1935).

During the ensuing hearings before the Subcommittee of the House on Interstate and Foreign Commerce, S. 5 was supported and criticized by practically the same groups as during the previous Senate hearings. The AMA and Consumers' Research wanted the bill more stringent; media owners and most advertising organizations wanted the bill passed; drug manufacturers urged that the FTC, rather than the FDA, be put in charge of any measure designed to regulate advertising of food, drugs, and cosmetics. *Printers' Ink* ("Reasonable and Fair," 1935), now speaking for the moderate majority, urged unity and stressed the need for a federal law on the books.

> It is perfectly obvious that some of these gentlemen [drug manufacturers] do not want any new law at all. ... If Moses himself could descend from Mount Sinai with a perfect measure it would be no more satisfying to them than was the fantastic Tugwell bill [S. 1944]. (p. 100)

Some suspected that endless debate over revisions and highly publicized hearings did not constitute the best form of public relations for the advertising industry. "Just between us," stated the president of the Advertising Federation of America, Edgar Kobak (1935), in a letter to NBC lobbyist Frank Russell, "the quicker we get a bill, the quicker the agitation against bad advertising will subside. Every time there is a hearing it makes swell publicity for men like Kallet" (p. 1). Industry leaders were eager to get the matter of permanent legislation resolved and have the topic removed from congressional—and public—consideration.

Consumer advocates held a different set of concerns. The numerous rewritings and amendments had resulted in a bill that was a far cry from the original Tugwell bill introduced 2 years earlier. As consumer protection ceased to be the central issue, the principal consumer groups were given only a limited role in the ensuing congressional deliberations, and they were almost entirely dissatisfied with the outcome. Consumers' Research, for example, claimed that anyone making a comparison between the original Tugwell bill and S. 5 could see that the bill no longer offered any protection for consumers and that it had, itself, been "adulterated and misbranded" (*Hearing Before a Subcommittee,* 1935, p. 506). At the House hearing in July and August 1935, Consumers' Research (*Hearing Before a Subcommittee,* 1935) cited "pressure from precisely the gentlemen who are guilty of all the other adulterations and misbranding" (p. 506) as the main force behind the bill's wording.

At the same time as S. 5 was sent to the House Committee on Interstate and Foreign Commerce for new hearings and a gamut of amendments and revisions, Senator David I. Walsh (Dem., MA) introduced a bill offering a new twist on the legislative matter. More than an amended Food and Drugs Act, the Walsh bill (S. 2909, 1935) placed regulatory power over advertising with the FTC rather than the FDA. It expanded the FTC's jurisdiction to crack down on misleading advertising, not only when it affected business competition but when such practices hurt consumers as well. A companion bill (H.R. 8744, 1935) was simultaneously introduced in the House of Representatives by Richard B. Russell, Jr. (Dem., GA; "Sixty Advertising Bills," 1935; "Walsh Bill," 1935).

THE FDA VERSUS THE FTC

S. 2909 brought to a head a simmering dispute over the proposed advertising legislation. The issue in the fall of 1935 was whether regulation set up in S. 5 should be directed by the FDA, as the Tugwell bill had authorized, or with the FTC. The fact that these two government bodies had a long competitive history complicated the issue. Judge Ewin L. Davis, head of the FTC, opposed giving FDA jurisdiction over false and misleading advertising. He argued that this constituted trespassing on the rights and duties of his commission to regulate unfair competition methods. False and misleading advertising, he maintained, was just another aspect of unfair competition. It made sense, according to Davis, that to avoid duplication of authority, his commission should also regulate misleading advertising practices. Davis proposed that S. 5 abandon all references to advertising regulation and that an amended version of the Federal Trade Commission Act leave this task to the FTC (Keyes, 1937).

Drug manufacturers came out in clear support of the FTC. The group had long feared that the FDA, which they thought boasted vigorous reformers with a clear antibusiness bias, would create severe obstacles for the drug industry ("S. 5 Evidence," 1935; Tedlow, 1981). They also believed that unlike the FDA, which was in a position to impose criminal sanctions and act quickly and decisively, the slow-working bureaucracy of the FTC, unimpressive sanctioning record, and limited power to impose punishments would prove less effective in dealing with violations under the proposed law. The support from the drug industry for the commission could also be read in light of the fact that the FTC had historically proven easier to manipulate than the FDA (Kolko, 1976; Tugwell, 1935a). However, not all elements of the advertising community agreed with the drug manufacturers. Although clearly resenting the FDA's interference with their business practices, large sections of the advertising industry were more apprehensive about the FTC quest for regulatory power, viewing the eagerness of the commission to gain such control as "power grabbing tactics [designed to gain] sweeping power over advertising and merchandising practices" ("Noisy and Troublesome," 1937, pp. 124–125).

Consumer advocates had a different set of objections to the FTC. They argued that the commission lacked the necessary testing facilities to determine false and misleading advertising properly and that, for this reason, it would prove quite ineffective in a regulatory capacity. The tendency of the commission toward slow procedures and mild penalties were concerns as well. Tugwell (1935b) wrote in a letter to Senator Bailey, who had emerged as a strong supporter of America's drug industries during the legislative battle.

> I do not approve the proposal that provisions against false advertising be enforced by the cease and desist order procedure of the Federal Trade Commission. This procedure is time consuming. It carries no penalty and has no deterrent effect on the evader and chiseler. (p. 1)

Consumer representatives were also suspicious of the eager endorsements bestowed on the FTC by conservative drug interests ("Women's Demands," 1937).

By now, discussions surrounding the food, drug, and cosmetic legislation centered entirely on the issue of whether the FDA or the FTC should regulate the new law. Consumer protection—the original focus and intent of the bill—was less frequently discussed and sometimes ridiculed. The Washington correspondent for *Printers' Ink* ("Pressure Groups," 1937) for example, blamed the "self appointed evangelists" (p. 12) of consumer spokesmen of having singled S. 5 out for attack just because it represented "a reasonably fairly practicable compromise under which enforcement agencies and affected industries may find it possible to function with a decent regard for the public interest" (p. 12). The trade journal argued that consumer advocates failed to represent the public's view on advertising regulation and accused them of using the pretense of consumer protection as a smokescreen for (unspecified) selfish interests. In the fall of 1936, the FTC officially recommended that the 1914 law be amended to give it broader powers over advertising ("Broadening of FTC's," 1936; "Trade Commission," 1936).

THE PASSAGE OF THE WHEELER–LEA AMENDMENTS

The new legislative focus was now on the Lea bill (H.R. 3143, 1937), an amended version of the 1914 Federal Trade Commission Act. The measure, introduced by Representative Clarence F. Lea (Dem., CA), gave the FTC control over all advertising in all media but delegated the job of enforcing technical phases such as labeling and packaging to the FDA. The Lea bill stipulated that an advertisement should be regarded as false when it misrepresented the character, quality, or therapeutic effect of an advertised commodity. The bill distinguished between advertisements that were false in a material respect and those that were injurious to consumers' health. It authorized cease-and-desist orders to deal with the former while allowing the FTC to seek injunctions against the latter. Representative Lea's (1937) measure entrusted the FTC with power over all "unfair or deceptive acts or practices" (p. 62) in commerce and gave it the right to exercise that power for the protection of consumers. The FTC was not expected to react with an injunction in every case of false advertising, however. Such involvement was limited to cases the commission determined to be "in the interest of the public" (p. 62). Unlike the Tugwell bill, which had intended to place the burden of proof with advertisers, the Lea bill placed the task of proving false and misleading advertising claims with the FTC. Although the bill proposed fines for dissemination of false advertising, it did not propose prison terms for such offenses ("F.T.C. to Rule Advertising," 1937).

The new measure allowed the FTC to police false and misleading advertising while leaving the FDA in charge of false and misleading branding and labels. This measure entrusted all regulatory power over advertising with the FTC and left the FDA with no more power over such marketing devices than it already held under the existing Pure Food and Drug Act ("Mr. Dunn Writes," 1937; "Predict Early Action," 1937; "Ready for Drug Bill," 1937). The Lea measure passed in the House June 1937. Around the same time, the Senate voted favorably on the Wheeler bill (S. 1077, 1937), a measure that, theoretically at least, was intended as a companion bill to the Lea measure (Pease, 1958; Tedlow, 1981).

After passing the vote, S. 1077 was sent to the House Interstate and Foreign Commerce Committee. This committee was chaired by Representative Lea, who feared that the Wheeler bill would have problems passing the House. Lea's strategy was to strike out the complete text of the Wheeler bill except for the title, substitute the text with the Lea bill, which had already been passed by the House, and report the bill out again as S. 1077. The bill was now referred to as the Wheeler–Lea bill. Although its text on food, drug, and cosmetic advertising was lifted from the food and drug provision in the Copeland bill (S. 5), the bill stipulated that jurisdiction over such advertising should rest with the FTC rather than the FDA (Lea, 1938; "Lea Bill," 1938; Miller, 1938). When the Wheeler–Lea bill went to conference, it was sent to the Senate Committee on *Interstate* Commerce [emphasis added], which was chaired by Senator Wheeler, rather than to the Senate Committee on Commerce chaired by Senator Copeland ("Lea Bill," 1938; McMillan, 1937). The Wheeler–Lea bill passed the House on a standing vote, 107 to 10, in January 1938 and was written into law later the same year ("New Advertising Bill," 1938). In September 1938, the law launched its first action against an advertiser ("FTC Launches," 1938).

Although trusting regulatory powers over advertising to the FTC, the Wheeler–Lea amendment to the Federal Trade Commission Act merely stated the parameters of the commission's jurisdiction. The new law had not solved the need for a revised version of the Food and Drug Act of 1906. A modified version of S. 5 proved to be a solution to the problem. This measure, written into law June 1938, amended the 1906 law but left advertising regulation of foods, drugs, and cosmetics out of the picture (Food, Drug, and Cosmetic Act, 1938; Pease, 1958; Witherspoon, 1998; Young, 1967/1992).

THE WHEELER–LEA AMENDMENTS
AND THEIR PRACTICAL IMPLICATIONS

The purpose behind the Wheeler–Lea amendments were to strengthen and supplement the Federal Trade Commission Act of 1914. The principal difference between the original (1914) and the amended act was an extension of the jurisdiction of the FTC to protect consumers as well as competitors against injuries resulting from deceptive acts and practices in interstate commerce (Thompson, 1938b). The new provisions were directed against two broad, general categories of business practices. One was the use of unfair methods of competition and unfair or deceptive acts or practices in commerce. The other was the use of false or misleading advertising of foods, drugs, devices, and cosmetics (Miller, 1938). As such, the amended law opened up a whole new arena for FTC activity. It gave the commission an opportunity to regain power and respect that had been whittled away in its attempts to regulate competition (Tedlow, 1981). The FTC was no longer limited to issuing cease-and-desist orders; now, in certain situations, it could impose penalties. The commission had also gained the long-desired right to intervene in cases where consumers' interests were at stake ("The Regulation of Advertising," 1956).

Consumer advocates were not enthusiastic about the benefits conferred by the new law, although in the depressed environment surrounding the passage of the law some, perhaps many, thought it better than nothing at all. They claimed that the law was "without teeth" and that merely issuing cease-and-desist orders would prove "absolutely ineffective" ("New Advertising Bill Passed," 1938, p. 17) in preventing false and misleading advertising from appearing in the first place. They also argued that the new ability of the FTC to impose penalties was too limited and that this prevented the commission from protecting the public from false and misleading advertising ("New Advertising Bill Passed," 1938).

Undeniably, the Wheeler–Lea amendment put the burden of proving the false or misleading nature of an advertisement on the government and not, as the Tugwell bill had insisted, on the advertiser. Advertising reformers understood that this powerful legal distinction would go a long way toward undermining the possibility of rigorous federal regulation of advertising. The FTC, at best, was left to prosecute false and misleading advertising after consumers already had been hurt ("Wheeler–Lea Bill," 1938). A survey conducted by the advertising industry in early 1940 revealed consumer discontent with the new law. Of the 5,000 people interviewed, 59% were in favor of further advertising regulations (Gallup, 1940).

The new set of legal restrictions were much milder than advertisers had first feared, and the law hardly affected the large majority of advertisers. Even *Printers'
Ink* ("The Food Bill Situation," 1937), which had long and consistently opposed the FTC's role as advertising administrator, had to admit that business could live with the law because there was "nothing particularly vicious" (p. 95) about it. Benson of

the AAAA, who had fought a 5-year battle to preserve advertisers' right to trade puffery shared these sentiments. He ("Coast Council Hears," 1938) described the new law as a "marvelous piece of legislation" (p. 19) that was likely to increase advertising's power in the future. Seemingly, the advertising community realized that, compared to some of the more stringent regulation proposals that had circulated in the years preceding passage of the Wheeler–Lea amendments, this law allowed them to breathe a deep sigh of relief.

Indeed, the new law presented little hardship for the vast majority of advertisers. During the first 2 years of the existence of the law, the FTC investigated slightly more than 800 new cases (Morehouse, 1940). Combined with cases that were pending before the amendments went into effect and a few cases that were reopened for future consideration, the commission investigated a total of 1,137 cases between March 1938 and May 1940 (Morehouse, 1940). In all, these resulted in a total of 17 injunctions and a single criminal prosecution that involved an abortifacient believed to seriously endanger the lives of those who used it; the latter resulted in a plea of guilty and a fine of $1,000 (Morehouse, 1940). Not surprisingly, this outcome encouraged *Advertising & Selling* (Rippey, 1940) to assure wary advertisers that the FTC did not believe in severe regulation of advertising.

The practical application of the new law proved that consumer advocates had been right in fearing that the new measure failed to provide consumers with any substantial protection against false and misleading advertising. The major shortcoming of the new law was its failure to encourage advertisers to provide more factual information in their ads. The immediate and somewhat ironic effect of the law on advertising copy was a tendency toward increasing glamour and indirect assertion. Because it was relatively easy to check the truthfulness of explicit written claims, advertisements increasingly relied on the use of pictures and illustrations to get around the law. Most advertising agencies were inspired to design copy that complied with the law yet served the purpose of techniques that the amended version of the Federal Trade Commission Act rendered illegal. Pease (1958) argued

It was obvious that a pictorial illustration could frequently pass muster where a verbal presentation would not, that a promise of reward as a result of purchasing the product could often be enhanced by being left unspecified and thereby innocent of legal transgression. (p. 132).

In sum, the Wheeler–Lea Act and the regulation it spawned were crowning achievements for the advertising industry, which was able to get favorable legislation passed and to have the issue effectively removed from congressional or public consideration thereafter. Nevertheless, the advertising industry knew it could never take the lax regulation by the FTC for granted. As an industry it was always susceptible to public criticism for its sometimes controversial operations, which might lead to increased FTC regulation, or even to Congress reopening the matter of advertising regulation for further consideration. Thus, the advertising industry had incentive to constantly lobby the White House, the FTC, and Congress to assure that the FTC never got too carried away with the notion of regulating advertising in the public interest. In this sense, the Wheeler–Lea amendments gave rise to the need for the advertising industry to have a permanent and prominent lobbying presence in Washington, just as commercial broadcasters, securities traders, and other regulated industries did. Recognizing that advertising regulation was favored by a substantial segment of the population, the advertising industry needed to keep a close ear to the ground to protect the status quo and nip new challenges in the bud (Stole, 1998).

CONCLUSIONS

Despite demands from consumer groups, New Dealers, and government regulatory agencies, advertisers survived the 5-year legislative battle over advertising regulation with surprising ease. Although both the Tugwell bill and the Wheeler–Lea amendments claimed to protect the consumer against false and misleading advertising, the two bills were drastically different. The former was drafted with consumer protection in mind; the latter reflected the successful 5-year effort by the advertising community to render such protection painless for business interests. This transformation reflected the supreme power of the lobby in Washington, DC by the advertising industry as well as its power to influence the public agenda through the commercial mass media.

From the perspective of consumers, the Wheeler–Lea amendments left an enormous gray area for advertising puffery; advertisers could mislead consumers even as they obeyed the letter of the law. Today, more than 6 decades later, consumers continue to suffer the consequences (Preston, 1994, 1996). To some extent, advertising puffery has escaped regulation because advertisers claim that this marketing device does not work. At the same time, and in a somewhat hypocritical manner, advertisers are frequent users of this sales technique because they know it does indeed work.

Maybe the time has once more come for consumers to demand that advertisers become directly responsible for their promotional claims. The U.S. policy of caveat emptor—let the buyer beware—has enjoyed a long and, for advertisers, quite lucrative run. Maybe the time has come to take cues from other countries like Finland, Thailand, and the Scandinavian nations, to mention a few. More inclined to place the burden of promotional truths with advertisers, these countries are excellent examples of how increased levels of consumer protection do not translate into commercial demise (Herbig, 1997; Morse, 1993, Preston, 1994).

It is possible to turn the U.S. tide, but there is definitely an urgency to the matter. In the past 25 years the advertising industry has won important cases before the U.S.

Supreme Court to the effect that commercial advertising is now increasingly protected from government regulation by the free speech clause in the First Amendment. It is not entirely unthinkable that at some point in the future, advertising will be made, in effect, part of the U.S. Constitution and thereby removed forever from the arena of public debate and regulation (McChesney, 1999). Unless we act soon, chances are that we will spend endless decades with ads that tell us too little and promise too much.

ACKNOWLEDGMENT

I thank Robert W. McChesney for his comments on earlier drafts of this article.

REFERENCES

Advertising and the U.S. (1933, November 30). *Printers' Ink*, 84.
Advertising—Brief survey and current status. (1939, March). *The Index, 19*(1), 15–21.
Advertising censorship reaches Congress. (1933, June 8). *Printers' Ink*, 82–83.
Advertising or Tugwell. (1933, October 28). *Business Week*, 14.
Ambiguity of Tugwell bill is criticized. (1933, October 28). *Advertising Age*, 8.
A.N.A. withholds approval of food, drug legislation. (1935, February 7). *Advertising Age*, 1.
Backs food and drug bill. (1933, November 16). *The New York Times*, p. 6.
Baran, P. A., & Sweezy, P. M. (1966). *Monopoly capital*. New York: Monthly Review.
Beatty, S. (1998, June 24). Forecast for '98 U.S. ad budgets. *The Wall Street Journal*, p. B5.
Broadening of FTC's power over competition is sought. (1936, December 15). *Advertising Age*, 12.
Christians, C. M., Fackler, M., Rotzoll, K., & McKee, K. (1997). *Media ethics: Cases and moral reasoning* (3rd ed.). New York: Longman.
Coast council hears Benson applaud Wheeler–Lea Act. (1938, October 31). *Advertising Age*, 19.
Coen, R. J. (1999). Spending spree. *Advertising Age*, 126.
*Commerce (S.2800): Hearings before the Committee of the United States Senate,*73rd Cong., 2d Sess. 194 (1934a) (testimony of J. A. Benson).
*Commerce (S.2800): Hearings before the Committee of the United States Senate,*73rd Cong., 2d Sess. 276 (1934b) (testimony of A. Kallet).
Commerce (S.2800): Hearings before the Committee of the United States Senate, 73rd Cong., 2d Sess. 409 (1934c) (testimony of J. Rorty).
Consumers in limelight at Copeland hearing. (1934, March 1). *Printers' Ink*, 20.
Copeland bill slated for quick passage. (1934, February 15). *Printers' Ink*, 21.
Curti, M. (1967). The changing concept of human nature in the literature of American advertising. *Business History Review, 41*, 334–357.
Drastic revisions made in new draft of Tugwell bill. (1934, January 6). *Advertising Age*, 1.
Drug act revision backed by women. (1933, November 17). *The New York Times*, p. 40.
Drug and yeast. (1933, December). *Tide*, 36.
Elliot, S. (1998, June 24). Advertising. *The New York Times*, p. C8.
The food bill situation. (1937, July 15). *Printers' Ink*, 95–96.
Food and Drug Act, 34 Stat. 768 (1906).
Food and drugs. (1933, May). *Tide*, 8–9.

Food, Drug, and Cosmetic Act, 21 U.S. Code §§ 301–392 (1938).

Food, drugs, and cosmetics (S.1944): Hearings before the Subcommittee on Commerce, 73rd Cong., 2d Sess. 83 (1934a) (testimony of J. H. Beal).

Food, drugs, and cosmetics (S.1944): Hearings before the Subcommittee on Commerce, 73rd Cong., 2d Sess. 330 (1934b) (testimony of J. A. Benson).

Food, drugs, and cosmetics (S.1944): Hearings before the Subcommittee on Commerce, 73rd Cong., 2d Sess. 456 (1934c) (testimony of E. Hanson).

Food, drugs, and cosmetics (S.1944): Hearings before the Subcommittee on Commerce, 73rd Cong., 2d Sess. 355 (1934d) (testimony of A. Kallet).

Food, drugs, and cosmetics (S.1944): Hearings before the Subcommittee on Commerce, 73rd Cong., 2d Sess. 312 (1934e) (testimony of C. C. Parlin).

Four food bills and all good. (1934, February 1). *Printers' Ink,* 69.

Fox, S. (1997). *The mirror makers: A history of American advertising and its creators.* Urbana/Chicago: University of Illinois Press. (Original work published 1984)

FTC launches first Wheeler–Lea action in court. (1938, September 19). *Advertising Age,* 4.

F.T.C. to rule advertising. (1937, July 15). *Printers' Ink,* 29.

Gallup, G. (1940, February 9). An analysis of the study of consumer agitation. Box 76, Folder 11, National Broadcasting Corporation papers. Wisconsin Center Historical Archives, State Historical Society of Wisconsin, Madison.

Harris, R. A., & Milkis, S. M. (1989). *The politics of regulatory change: A tale of two agencies.* New York: Oxford University Press.

Hedges, W. (1933, November 6). Letter to Royal. Box 22, Folder 37, National Broadcasting Corporation papers. Wisconsin Center Historical Archives, State Historical Society of Wisconsin, Madison.

Herbig, P. A. (1997). *Handbook of cross-cultural marketing.* New York: International Business Press.

Hodges, G. (1934, April 19). Advertising must fight as well as clean up. *Printers' Ink,* 33.

H.R. 3143, 75th Cong., 1st Sess. (1937).

H.R. 8316, 73rd Cong., 2nd Sess. (1934).

H.R. 8744, 74th Cong., 1st Sess. (1935).

Interstate and foreign commerce (HR.6906; HR 8805; HR.8941; S.5): Hearings before the Subcommittee of the House of Representatives, 74th Cong., 1st Sess. 505 (1935) (testimony of J. B. Matthews).

Is the Tugwell bill an administrative measure? (1933, December 30). *Advertising Age,* 4.

Is U.S. against advertising? (1933, November 2). *Printers' Ink,* 100.

Jacobs, W. P. (1933, November 17). Letter to Aylesworth. Box 22, Folder 37, National Broadcasting Corporation papers. Wisconsin Center Historical Archives, State Historical Society of Wisconsin, Madison.

Jacobson, M. F., & Mazur, L. A. (1995). *Marketing madness: A survival guide for consumer society.* Boulder CO: Westview.

The Joint Committee for Sound and Democratic Consumer Legislation. (n.d.). A statement of vital interest to all who desire to maintain and protect the American system. Box 32, Folder 70, National Broadcasting Corporation papers. Wisconsin Center Historical Archives, State Historical Society of Wisconsin, Madison.

Kallet, A. (1934a, January 27). Letter to Bassin. Box 3, Folder 9, Arthur Kallet papers. Center for the Study of the Consumer Movement, Yonkers, NY.

Kallet, A. (1934b, March 3). Letter to S[chlink]. Box 3, Folder 9, Arthur Kallet papers. Center for the Study of the Consumer Movement, Yonkers, NY.

Kallet, A., & Schlink, F. J. (1933). *100,000,000 Guinea pigs.* New York: Vanguard.

Keyes, E. R. (1937, February 11). The Federal Trade Commission's police record. *Advertising & Selling,* 25.

Kobak, E. (1935, March 13). Memo to Russell. Box 35, Folder 47, National Broadcasting Corporation papers. Wisconsin Center Historical Archives, State Historical Society of Wisconsin, Madison.

Kolko, G. (1976). *Main currents in modern American history.* New York: Harper & Row.

Last roundup. (1933, November). *Tide,* 44.

Lea bill passes house. (1938, January 20). *Printers' Ink,* 24–26.

Lea, C. F. (1937, August 15). Would the FTC's purge for advertising cure the patient or kill it? *Sales Management,* 62–64.

Lea, C. F. (1938, May). Congressman Lea reviews his law. *Advertising & Selling,* 21.

Lynd, R. S. (1934, May). The consumer becomes a "problem." *The Annals of the America Academy, 173,* 1–6.

Marchand, R. (1985). *Advertising the American dream: Making way for modernity, 1920–1945.* Berkeley: University of California Press.

McAllister, M. P. (1996). *The commercialization of American culture: New advertising, control and democracy.* Thousand Oaks, CA: Sage.

McChesney, R. W. (1993). *Telecommunications, mass media and democracy: The battle for control of U.S. broadcasting, 1928–1935.* New York: Oxford University Press.

McChesney, R. W. (1999). *Rich media, poor democracy: Communications policies in dubious times.* Urbana: University of Illinois Press.

McMillan, G. S. (1937, December 16). Much advertising "regulation" in prospect; 60 bills now before Congress. *Printers' Ink,* 11–13.

Miller, H. (1938, April 1). A new and stronger advertising statute. *Broadcasting,* 19.

Morehouse, P. B. (1940, May). After two years of Wheeler–Lea. *Advertising & Selling,* 22–23.

Morse, R. L. D. (1993). *The consumer movement: Lectures by Colston E. Warne.* Manhattan, KS: Family Economics Trust.

Mott, F. L. (1962). *American journalism* (3rd ed.). New York: MacMillan.

Mr. Dunn writes to Mr. Lea. (1937, May 27). *Printers' Ink,* 64.

N.P.A. "Tugwell committee" lays down platform. (1933, December 9). *Advertising Age,* 9.

National Association of Broadcasters Reports. (1934a, January 6). p. 267.

National Association of Broadcasters Reports. (1934b, February 19). p. 299.

New advertising bill passed by House. (1938, January 15). *Broadcasting,* 17.

Nichols, G. A. (1934, January 11). It is the Copeland bill now. *Printer's Ink,* 69.

Nine objections to the Tugwell bill—With their answers. (1933, November 23). *Advertising & Selling,* 13–15.

Noisy and troublesome. (1937, January 21). *Printers' Ink,* 124–125.

Pease, O. (1958). *The responsibilities of American advertising: Private control and public influence, 1920–1940.* New Haven: Yale University Press.

Predict early action on remodeled Lea bill. (1937, July 12). *Advertising Age,* 1.

Pressure groups revive. (1937, January 21). *Printers' Ink,* 12.

Preston, I. L. (1994). *The tangled web they weave: Truth, falsity & advertisers.* Madison: University of Wisconsin Press.

Preston, I. L. (1996). *The great American blowup: Puffery in advertising and selling.* Madison: University of Wisconsin Press.

Proprietary association president answers Tugwell on new drug bill. (1933, October 9). *Oil, Paint and Drug Reporter,* 15.

Publishers of the Evening Tribune. (1933, December 28). Telegram to Roosevelt. Box 375, Folder Tugwell PFA 1933–35, Franklin D. Roosevelt papers. The President's Official Files, Franklin D. Roosevelt Library, Hyde Park, NY.

Pure Food and Drug Act of 1906, Ch. 3915 34 Stat. 768 (1906).

Ready for drug bill "solution." (1937, June 12). *Business Week,* 25–26.

Reasonable and fair. (1935, December 19). *Printers' Ink,* 100.

The regulation of advertising. (1956, November). *Columbia Law Review, 56,* 1019–1111.

Rippey, S. (1940, February). The FTC in unofficial profile. *Advertising & Selling,* 20–22.

Rorty, J. (1976). *Our master's voice: Advertising.* New York: Arno. (Original published 1934)

S. 1077, 75th Cong., 1st Sess. (1937).

S. 1944, 73rd Cong., 2nd Sess. (1934).

S. 2000, 73rd Cong., 2nd Sess. (1934).

S. 2800, 73rd Cong., 2nd Sess. (1934).

S. 2909, 74th Cong., 1st Sess. (1935).

S. 5, 74th Cong., 1st Sess. (1935).

S. 5 evidence is in. (1935, March 14). *Printers' Ink,* 27–28.

Savan, L. (1994). *The sponsored life: Ads, TV and American culture.* Philadelphia: Temple University Press.

Scientific Consumer Purchasing. (1934–1935). Box 10, Folder CAB Correspondence (General) A, National Recovery Administration—Consumer Division. General File of the Consumers' Advisory Board, 1934–1935. Record Group 9. National Archives, Washington DC.

Schlink, F. J. (1933a, March 7). Letter to Tugwell. Box 6, Folder Consumers' Research, Rexford Tugwell papers. Franklin D. Roosevelt Library, Hyde Park, NY.

Schlink, F. J. (1933b, May 26). Letter to Tugwell. Box 6, Folder Consumers' Research, Rexford Tugwell papers. Franklin D. Roosevelt Library, Hyde Park, NY.

Self regulation under the Tugwell bill? (1934, January 6). *Advertising Age,* 4.

Six bills: Take your choice. (1934, March 8). *Printers' Ink,* 33–34.

Sixty advertising bills. (1935, September 12). *Printers' Ink,* 7.

Stole, I. L. (1998). *Selling advertising: The U.S. advertising industry and its public relations strategies, 1932–1945.* Unpublished doctoral dissertation, University of Wisconsin, Madison.

Thompson, J. W. (1938a, October 25). Confidential memo. Box 7, Folder 4, J. Walter Thompson Archives. Duke University, NC.

Thompson, J. W. (1938b, May 9). Important JWT forum. Box 7, Folder 4, J. Walter Thompson Archives. Duke University, NC.

Tedlow, R. (1981). From competitor to consumer: The changing focus of federal regulation of advertising, 1914–1938. *Business History Review, 55*(1), 35–58.

Trade commission will seek direct advertising control. (1936, November 16). *Advertising Age,* 1.

Tug-o-war. (1933, October). *Tide,* 20–21.

Tugwell bill center of attention as hearings open. (1933, December 7). *Advertising & Selling,* 18.

Tugwell bill is target of bitter attack. (1933, October 14). *Advertising Age,* 1.

Tugwell, G. R. (1934, February 21). Letter to Roosevelt, Box 375, Folder Tugwell PFA 1933–1935, Franklin D. Roosevelt papers. The President's Official Files, Franklin D. Roosevelt Library, Hyde Park, NY.

Tugwell, G. R. (1935a, January 24). Letter to Richberg, Box 375, Folder Tugwell PFA 1933–1935, Franklin D. Roosevelt papers. The President's Official Files, Franklin D. Roosevelt Library, Hyde Park, NY.

Tugwell, G. R. (1935b, April 26). Letter to Bailey, Box 375, Folder Tugwell PFA 1933–1935, Franklin D. Roosevelt papers. The President's Official Files, Franklin D. Roosevelt Library, Hyde Park, NY.

Veblen, T. (1938). *The engineers and the price system.* New York: Viking. (Original work published 1921)

Veblen, T. (1954). *Absentee ownership and business enterprise in recent times: The case of America.* New York: Viking. (Original work published 1923)

Walsh bill. (1935, June 6). *Printers' Ink,* 25–26.

Wheeler–Lea Act, 15 U.S. Code § 41, 44, 45, 52–58 (1938).

Wheeler–Lea bill broadening powers of FTC over advertising is now law. (1938, April 1). *Broadcasting,* 18.

Why all advertisers are interested in the Tugwell bill. (1933, October 21). *Advertising Age,* 4.

Witherspoon, E. M. (1998). Courage of conviction: *The St. Louis Post-Dispatch, The New York Times,* and reform of the Pure Food and Drug Act, 1933–1937. *Journalism and Mass Communication Quarterly, 75,* 776–788.

Women's demands delay Lea bill. (1937, June 3). *Printers' Ink,* 14.

Young, J. H. (1992). *The medical messiahs: A social history of health quackery in the twentieth century America.* Princeton, NJ: Princeton University Press. (Original work published 1967)

Consumer Culture and Television Home Shopping Programming: An Examination of the Sales Discourse

Judi Puritz Cook

Communications Program
Salem State College

In this article, I examine television home shopping programs to explore how social class issues are incorporated into the discourse of selling products. More specifically, a content analysis of the 3 major home shopping cable channels—Home Shopping Network, Quality–Value–Convenience, and Q2—is conducted. I argue that home shopping programming, in general, addresses social class issues through the identification of financial limitations, the promise of status mobility through consumption, and the fostering of anxiety with regard to one's social standing. This research contributes to the larger theory pertaining to social-order maintenance. In this article, I suggest that consumption on home shopping is offered as one means of resolving class tensions among the haves and have nots. More specifically, I argue not only that material consumption may be sold as a means to dispel class antagonism and anxiety but that home shopping programming addresses class-appropriate ideological discourse.

A caller phones the on-air host at Quality–Value–Convenience (QVC) during the sale of a 14 karat gold ring embedded with imitation diamonds. She says to the host of the program, "Thanks to you and QVC, we [the viewers] are able to look rich, so to speak."[1] With a knowing smile to the camera, host Kathy Levine agrees and adds, "You really, really look like you're wearing a $10,000 ring here. This is a top quality color of the diamond … a great rendition of what should be an unbelievably expensive ring."[2]

Requests for reprints should be sent to Judi Puritz Cook, Communications Program, Salem State College, 352 Lafayette Street, Salem, MA 01970. E-mail: judi@puritz.com

[1]Anonymous caller, Quality–Value–Convenience, June 29, 1997.
[2]Kathy Levine, Quality–Value–Convenience, June 29, 1997.

This example illustrates a typical sales pitch on a home shopping channel. Hosts and callers interact to create a frenzied atmosphere designed to goad viewers into making purchases. As a form of advertising, the technique of appealing to consumers' potential needs for status mobility through consumption is not new. However, I argue that there is more at work than a simple case of home shopping serving as another vehicle to promote consumerism. Closer observation of the home shopping channels suggests the rhetoric of home shopping speaks to social class ideology.

In this article, I examine television home shopping to explore how issues of class identification, class mobility, and class anxiety are manifested in the discourse of selling products to viewers. More specifically, a content analysis of the three major home shopping cable channels, Home Shopping Network (HSN), QVC, and the now-defunct Q2, is conducted to determine the extent to which home shopping discourse reveals how the social class of consumers is identified, sustained, and challenged while products are sold.

Perhaps of all television fare, home shopping programming is typically viewed as sociologically simple, that is, as programming with little value other than to engage and promote consumerism. Consequently, there is a relative dearth of research devoted to home shopping. This is not to say that home shopping programming has not been studied or considered worthy of scholarly attention. Scholarship on the television home shopping channels has addressed issues such as media system dependency (Grant, Gutherie, & Ball-Rokeach, 1991), the function of television shopping as it relates to the commercialization of culture (McAllister, 1996), parasocial interaction between on-air personalities and viewers (Auter & Moore, 1993), the transformation of the marketplace (Gumpert & Drucker, 1992), and critical analysis of class and gender messages (White, 1995). However, the amount of scholarly attention given to these channels is scant when one considers the reach and strength of these channels—home shopping networks have been in operation for more than 14 years and often run 24 hours a day, 7 days a week, reaching an estimated 120 million households (Corporate Facts, 1996; Landler, 1996).

This research, then, attempts to treat this popular programming as providing symbolic values beyond simple consumerism. More specifically, it can be argued that home shopping programming reflects an awareness of the social class of its audiences. Moreover, that awareness acknowledges economic limitations (when necessary) and simultaneously fosters what may be called class anxiety or, more specifically, working-class anxiety. This anxiety refers to working-class discomfort with its lower social standing, its corollary desire for upward social mobility, and the tension resulting from this discomfort and desire (see Dobriner, 1963; Fallers, 1966; Laumann, 1966; Marchand, 1985; Packard, 1959; Veblen, 1899; Warner, Meeker, & Eells, 1970). More intriguingly, perhaps, home shopping discourse may also propose how consumption may resolve this tension between class limitations and aspirations. For viewers, "home shopping promises ... the lives of the rich, the famous, the glamorous—on the cheap, and just a phone call away" (Waldman,

1995, p. 12). Such an illusion may appease members of lower classes by allowing them to believe they have achieved status mobility when in fact they have not (Fallers, 1966; Marchand, 1985).

In aggregate, this development of both tension and remedy can be related to the larger issue of social-order maintenance (Goldman, 1992; Leiss, Kline, & Jhally, 1990; Thomas, 1986). As explained by Leiss et al. in the following:

> Many writers also claim that advertising plays a more straightforward role in transmitting an ideology that perpetuates the status quo and its exploitative social relations, through the presentation of a world view that encourages the audience to interpret reality in ways that work to the benefit of those who already possess the power. (pp. 31–32)

Thomas (1986) argued that mass media discourse generally serves to quell class antagonisms by portraying vast possibilities for upward social mobility alongside grim and cynical portrayals of that mobility once achieved. Home shopping discourse may be seen as contributing to the same general process although presenting somewhat different strategies and arguments. Although home shopping programming does not necessarily offer grim portrayals of wealthy people, it presents a different dialectic between the economic circumstances facing working-class viewers and appeals for upward mobility through consumption. In some ways, appearing to have material wealth is portrayed as more desirable than actually possessing material wealth: The former circumstance allows for consumers to be smart with their purchases. A sales pitch on QVC illustrates this point best:

> My attitude is, I'm a smart gal, why would I spend all my money in diamonds when I can buy Diamonique from QVC? I can have all the flash, I can have all the brilliance, all the look I want. I can look like those ladies worth a zillion dollars, but I haven't spent a zillion dollars to get that look.[3]

At its most obvious, home shopping programming promotes capitalism by engaging in it: As viewers materially engage in home shopping, the system is fed, and the working viewer is, to varying extents, financially depleted. Furthermore, making purchases allows viewers to possess items that, according to the promise of home shopping, create the illusion of mobility. To the extent that the signs purchased on home shopping seem to fulfill for buyers the class conditions they seek, it can be argued that home shopping programming provides a conservative influence by fostering willing compliance with the extant social structure. Therefore, through a systematic study of the sales discourse of home shopping and, in particular, a comparison between the discourse of general-audience programming (as on HSN

---

[3]Suzanne Runyan, Quality–Value–Convenience, June 28, 1997.

and QVC) and programming aimed at an upscale audience (Q2), the relation between class ideology and television home shopping can be examined.

Certainly, one may think of television commercials in relation to a study of home shopping. However, home shopping programming is different from commercials on two levels. First, home shopping is interactive—engaging the viewer and inviting participation. Second, home shopping programming is just that—programming. Although commercials may be analyzed as miniprograms of sorts, they are institutionally defined as something entirely separate and distinct.

Ironically, class and economic symbolism are rarely variables in the study of advertisements on television. In *Undressing the Ad*, Valdivia (1997) confirmed that little is said about advertising and the working class: "However, this omission is very logical since it makes little sense to represent a class that is below the levels of consumption to which we are supposed to aspire" (p. 228). Valdivia argued that many advertisers target the working class, knowing this portion of the population has money to spend.

Regarding regular television programming, social class representations have, of course, been studied (e.g., Berk, 1977; Butsch, 1992; Butsch & Glennon, 1980; Gentile & Miller, 1961; Thomas & Callahan, 1982). Virtually all this extant scholarship analyzed the more obvious social class imaging in fiction or (less likely) in news media. This research adds the dimension of home shopping programming as an alternative and important genre in the contribution of the media to social-order maintenance.

In sum, I attempt to answer two central questions. First, is there a sales discourse identifying and differentially addressing viewers' social class? This can be determined by comparing the discourse of Q2, on one hand, with HSN and QVC, on the other. Second, to what extent can home shopping discourse generally be interpreted as economic ideology? That is, beyond the mere selling of items, can it be said that the home shopping networks offer discourse on important matters concerning money, stature, and wealth?

THE MAJOR HOME SHOPPING NETWORKS

HSN went on air in 1985, with QVC following only a year behind. Emerging with a slow start, home shopping grew to be a $2 billion industry in 1993 (Zinn, DeGeorge, Shortez, Jones, & Anderson Forest, 1993). In 1995, sales at QVC alone reached $1.6 billion as the station logged more than 70 million phone orders and shipped more than 46 million packages (Corporate Facts, 1996). Presently, both HSN and QVC broadcast 24 hours a day, 7 days a week.

HSN reaches 66 million households through a combination of cable and broadcast distribution (Landler, 1996). QVC reaches over 54 million cable homes in the United States and introduces 250 new products to viewing audiences every week (Corporate Facts, 1996). In 1993, QVC introduced the Q2 channel in an attempt to reach a more upscale market (Donaton, 1993). Q2 was broadcast live 18 hours a day, 7 days a week, often selling the daily best sellers at QVC to 11 million cable homes (Corporate Facts, 1996).

Q2 was targeted to a smaller market of television viewers—11 million compared to 54 million at QVC (Corporate Facts, 1996). It went off the air in 1998 after QVC decided the spin-off channel was no longer profitable (Petrozzello, 1998). Interestingly, Q2 was developed ostensibly to attract those viewers who had looked down on home shopping (Donaton, 1993; Corporate Facts, 1996). However, it is difficult to say if QVC was aiming the Q2 channel at an upscale market. Q2 denied that they were seeking a more affluent market and instead positioned the Q2 channel as a time saver for busy shoppers (Corporate Facts, 1996; Donaton, 1993). "Q2 is chasing a life-style, seeking active adults who are juggling the demands of career, family and shrinking leisure time and have little patience for weekend trips to the mall" (Donaton, 1993, p. 12). Although the Q2 channel denied targeting an upscale market, its president described the average Q2 shopper as young and affluent, with an individual income of $40,000 or more (Underwood, 1994).

If Q2 was indeed just a faster way to get to the best-selling items at QVC, one would expect to find the same types of appeals on Q2 as on the traditional home shopping channels. Therefore, one goal of this study was to determine if Q2 had different class appeals than QVC and HSN. Such a result would support the argument that home shopping executives are very much aware of the social class standings of viewers and that they play on class anxieties to sell products.

METHOD

The channels comprising major, nationally disseminated home shopping programming were analyzed. A sample of HSN, QVC, and Q2 was drawn over a 2-week period from April 11 through April 25, 1997. This time period most accurately represents the typical programming offered on home shopping in that it was not influenced by a seasonal event (e.g., Valentine's Day, Mother's Day, St. Patrick's Day). A rotated schedule was employed, based on 2-hour time blocks, to constitute a total of 72 hours. If at the end of a 2-hour time block a product was being sold, coding continued until the next item was introduced. Such a schedule was preferred to guarantee that the sample included the same variety of items sold on any given home shopping day.

The discourse surrounding all products was analyzed. Programs related to anything other than home shopping, commercials (i.e., self-promoting clips for the channels), scheduling announcements, and previews were excluded from the sample.

In coding each item up for sale, the following issues were systematically analyzed (although not all are detailed in this article due to space limitations): the item being sold (type, price, and characteristics); the sales force involved; the callers who were aired in connection to the sale; and, most important, the discourse regarding the product. Sales discourse was organized into the following categories: general aesthetic terms, body-related terms (i.e., language specifically centering on the ability of a product to improve one's look physically; e.g., "slimming"), gender-related terms, terms related to financial prudence, terms related to the notion of achieving upward mobility, trend-setting terms, and trend-following terms.

This analysis provided for systematically collected data that can be quantified. Many variables in the coding instrument provided directly an exhaustive list of values or choices. However, inasmuch as improvised discourse was also analyzed for many variables the coding instrument allowed for open-ended values. For example, when coding for trend-setting discourse, coders were asked to include any terms or phrases (in addition to those provided on the form) they thought illustrated this category. These additions included references to an item that was "cutting edge." Also, inasmuch as this investigation considered relative emphasis in addition to the range of discourse categories, the instrument coded the frequency with which various terms and phrases were invoked. All values resulting from this heuristic technique were subsequently integrated into a quantifiable coding scheme. Beyond this, the qualitative records also provided concrete illustrations for use in the discussion of the quantitative results.

Reliability for each variable was calculated using Krippendorf's (1980) coincidence matrix formula. Items with a reliability level of 0.70 and above were accepted for analysis.[4]

RESULTS

Types of Products

Five-hundred and eighty-two items were analyzed. Table 1 identifies the frequency of the various products sold. The top three categories (jewelry, women's

---

[4]The variables of time slot, channel, starting price, educated consumer, work hard for money, slenderizing, sexy, general physical improvement, feminine, and unisex each had a reliability level of 1.00. The reliability level for both item number and item type was 0.99. The reliability level for both price lowered and trend following was 0.98. The reliability level for both reference to a gift and various social uses was 0.96. The variables upward-mobility terms and general aesthetic terms had reliability levels of 0.95. The reliability level for the variables versatility of season and easy to care for was 0.94. The variable versatility of style had a reliability level of 0.93. The variables reference to a bargain and trend-setting terms both had a reliability level of 0.91. The reliability level for both seconds and various manipulations was 0.90. The variables reference to a limited quantity and versatility of color both had a reliability level of 0.89. The reliability level for the variable affordable was 0.82. The reliability level for the variable people will be envious was 0.81.

TABLE 1
Frequency of Product Type

Product Type	N	% of Sample
Jewelry	197	33.8
Clothes: women's	59	10.1
Fashion accessories	58	10.0
Collectibles	39	6.7
Cosmetics	34	5.8
Dolls	24	4.1
Home improvement	21	3.6
Electronics	18	3.1
Toys	16	2.7
Bed–bath	15	2.6
Exercise equipment	15	2.6
Kitchen items	15	2.6
Health aids–vitamins	14	2.4
Cooling systems	12	2.1
Miscellaneous	45	7.8
Totals	582	100.0

clothes, and fashion accessories) accounted for approximately 54% of all items coded. Collectible items (6.7%), cosmetics (5.8%), dolls (4.1%), home improvement items (3.6%), and electronics (3.1%) were the next most popular items. Toys, bed and bath items, exercise equipment, kitchen items, health aids, and cooling systems each made up between 2.1 and 2.7% of the products sold. The remaining products (e.g., food, furniture, tools, etc.) were less prevalent (each under 2.0%). These miscellaneous items made up a total of 7.8% ($N = 45$) of the products sold.

In considering the types of products sold on home shopping channels in general, it was a compelling finding that well over half the items presented on these shows were jewelry, clothes, cosmetics, or fashion accessories. Such a result also illustrates how home shopping is primarily a gendered form of programming. This makes sense given that our culture designates women as primary consumers. Furthermore, these items are things that people (more specifically, female consumers) show to the world. In this sense, the home shopping channels can be said to concentrate on products involving image creation. This finding is in line with Ewen's (1988) observation that the "powers of appearance" (p. 259) are central in commerce (and, following Ewen, 1988, every aspect of life).

Item types were collapsed into more general categories and organized according to channel (see Table 2). A chi-square test comparing the items sold on QVC, Q2, and HSN was statistically significant, $\chi^2(12, N = 582) = 133.7, p = .000$ (see Table 2). Q2 sold the most items in the electronics–home improvement–office category

TABLE 2
Analyses of Product Type and Channel

Product Type	QVC		Q2		HSN	
	N	%	N	%	N	%
Jewelry	87	42.2	60	30.3	50	28.1
Clothing–cosmetics–fashion accessories	70	34.0	18	9.1	64	36.0
Electronics–home improvement–office– entertainment	5	2.4	55	27.8	37	20.8
Kitchen–bed–bath	14	6.8	14	7.1	12	6.7
Collectibles–dolls	18	8.7	7	3.5	14	7.8
Exercise–health–sporting goods	8	3.9	25	12.6	1	0.6
Miscellaneous	4	1.9	19	9.6	0	0.0
Totals	206	100.0	198	100.0	178	100.0

Note. $\chi^2(12, N = 582) = 133.912, p = .000$.

and offered hardly any items in the clothing–cosmetics–fashion accessories category. QVC and HSN sold more products from the clothing–cosmetics–fashion accessories category. There was also a difference with regard to exercise equipment–health aids–sporting goods, a category that accounted for 12.6% of all Q2 items, 3.9% of QVC items, and 0.6% of HSN items.

Although the three channels had a great deal in common with regard to item types, they also had some significant differences. The majority of items sold on QVC and HSN could be classified as the image items listed previously. Q2, on the other hand, offered far fewer items in the jewelry, clothing, cosmetics, and accessory categories combined. Instead, the Q2 channel sold more items such as electronics, computers, sporting goods, and entertainment products. Understanding Q2 as an upscale network makes sense in light of this disparity: It may be less socially relevant to sell image to those already in the relatively more powerful positions. The appeal of image creation may be greater or more salient to the more underclass audiences for QVC and HSN.

Sales Discourse

In considering the discourse involved for selling different products, the majority of items in our sample contained references to financial prudence (71.5%). General aesthetic terms were also prevalent, with 54.6% of the items in the sample sold with such references. Thirty-four percent of the items in the sample evoked references to upward mobility. Trend-following (30.2%), trend-setting (16.7%), body-related (10.3%), and gender-related (6.9%) terminology was also present to a lesser degree (for frequency counts, see Table 3).

Space considerations do not allow for a detailed analysis of all sales discourse variables. For this reason, only the two most relevant types of sales discourse, those relating to financial prudence and upward mobility, are further explored.

Financial prudence. This section discusses references to the economic and utilitarian functions of the products—language that may be said to take financial limitations into consideration. This language included references to items at a bargain price; suggestions for various manipulations; suggestions for various social uses; versatility of color, season, or style; affordable items; and ease of care. Discourse that valorized financial limitation and pragmatism, such as being an educated consumer or working hard for one's money, was also coded. Of the 582 items in the sample, 416 contained references to financial prudence. When multiple utterances on a single item were considered, 1,393 words were classified in this category. These findings suggest that the home shopping channels do make overt references to the material considerations and financial limitations of viewers. Table 4 presents an overview of the frequencies for terms related to financial prudence.

A chi-square test showed a significant difference across the three channels, $\chi^2(2, N = 416) = 19.418, p = .000$, with regard to the presence of financial prudence variables. QVC (78.6%, $N = 162$) and HSN (75.8%, $N = 135$) had almost equal percentages of terms relating to financial prudence. A slightly smaller percentage of products at Q2 (60.1%, $N = 119$) were sold using terms related to financial prudence.

The significantly higher number of references to financial prudence on QVC and HSN and that Q2 would rely less on this selling technique is in keeping with expectations. However, the fact that more than half the items sold on the Q2 channel were sold with references to financial prudence suggests that, in general, such references are a common occurrence in home shopping across the board. No other variable in this study was as prevalent for all three channels.

Further chi-square analyses conducted on the financial prudence variables showed a significant difference with regard to product type, $\chi^2 (6, N = 416) =$

TABLE 3
Frequency of Sales Discourse Variables

Sales Discourse	No. of Items	%
Financial prudence	416	71.5
General aesthetic	318	54.6
Upward mobility	201	34.5
Trend following	176	30.2
Limited quantities	164	28.2
Trend setting	97	16.7
Body related	60	10.3
Gender related	40	6.9

TABLE 4
Overall Frequency of Terms Relating to Financial Prudence

Term	N	%
Reference to the bargain	439	31.5
Various manipulations	290	20.8
Many social uses	222	15.9
Reference to a gift	199	14.3
Versatility of style	67	4.8
Versatility of color	56	4.0
Affordable	43	3.1
Easy to care for	40	2.9
Versatility of season	24	1.7
Educated consumer	9	0.7
Working hard for your money	4	0.3
Totals	1,393	100.0

TABLE 5
Analyses of Financial Prudence and Product

Product Category	N	% Within Product
Jewelry	170	86.3
Clothing–cosmetics–accessories	126	82.9
Electronics–home improvement–office	45	46.4
Collectibles–dolls	25	64.1
Kitchen–bed–bath	22	55.0
Miscellaneous	14	60.9
Exercise–health–sporting goods	14	41.2
Total	416	100.0

Note. $\chi^2(6, N = 416) = 83.823, p = .000.$

83.823, $p = .000$ (see Table 5). Over 80% of the items in the jewelry and cloth-ing–cosmetics–accessories categories contained terms relating to financial pru-dence. Although mention of terms classified as financially prudent occurred for other products such as collectibles–dolls (64%), kitchen–bath (55%), electron-ics–home improvement–office (46.4%) and exercise–health–sporting goods (41.2%), the product categories for jewelry and clothing–cosmetics–accessories contained significantly more references.

Such findings suggest that items associated with personal image are importantly connected to sales rhetoric on financial pragmatism. For example, much of the jew-elry and clothing sold on home shopping channels was sold based on the claim that it was a bargain. In fact, references to "the bargain" ($N = 439$) were the most preva-lent terms relating to financial prudence. It appears that improving one's image is desirable, especially if it can be done in a frugal and cost-effective manner. However, the message about saving money was quite clear: You save so you can spend more. For example, one host encouraged viewers to buy a sterling cut amethyst ring for $28.93 with the following pitch:

> Why not save a few dollars? We're always looking for ways to save, and maybe you can find a way to use those extra dollars that you save and put it towards a coordinating pair of earrings, or a pendant or maybe even a bracelet.[5]

To determine if items discussed with reference to financial prudence were less expensive than other items, a one-way analysis of variance was conducted for the ending price of all items with regard to the financial prudence variable, $F(1, 576) = 4.261$, $p = .039$. Items classified as addressing financial prudence had a significantly lower mean price ($65.24 vs. $81.83).

Upward mobility. Although 201 of the 582 items contained references to upward mobility, the upward-mobility category included 498 total utterances due to multiple references (for frequencies, see Table 6). The following statement is an example of a sales pitch coded as upward mobility: "This looks like something you'd see Princess Diana wearing, or, you know, someone of very high stature."[6]

The terms *classy* and *classical* were mentioned most frequently, accounting for 15.5% of all upward-mobility terms. The second most popular term in this group was *elegant,* accounting for 14.9% in this category. Other terms included *made in Europe* (10.2%), *rich* (7.4%), *expensive looking* (7.2%), *extravagant* (6.6%), *looks like an heirloom or estate jewelry* (6.0%), *looks like a real diamond* (5.2%), *exquisite* (3.6%), *high end* (3.0%), *upgraded or upscale* (2.2%), and *look or feel like a million bucks* (2.2%). The remaining upward-mobility terms, ranging from *tasteful* to *sophisticated,* represented less than 2.0% of this category.

A chi-square test showed a significant difference across the three channels, $\chi^2(2, N = 201) = 18.514$, $p = .000$, with regard to the presence of any upward-mobility variables. QVC (40.8%, $N = 84$) and HSN (40.4%, $N = 72$) had almost an equal percentage of upward-mobility terms. A smaller percentage of products at Q2 (22.7%, $N = 45$) were sold using terms related to upward mobility.

These data are predictable and very much in keeping with the earlier discussion of product type. Again, upward mobility need not be sold as much to those who have already attained it. Clearly, upward-mobility references are more appropriate to the more working-class orientations of HSN and QVC, if, as suggested in the introduction, home shopping shows instill or reinforce a working-class anxiety alongside its corollary, celebration of material wealth.

---

[5]Jill Bauer, Quality–Value–Convenience, June 28, 1997.
[6]Lynn Murphy, Home Shopping Network, June 28, 1997.

TABLE 6
Overall Frequency of Terms Relating to Upward Mobility

Term	N	%
Classical–classy	77	15.5
Elegant	74	14.9
Made in Europe	51	10.2
Rich	37	7.4
Expensive looking	36	7.2
Extravagant	33	6.6
Looks like heirloom–antique–estate jewelry	30	6.0
Looks like a real diamond	26	5.2
Exquisite	18	3.6
High end	15	3.0
Upgraded–upscale	11	2.2
Feel or look like a million bucks	11	2.2
Luxurious	10	2.1
Designer	10	2.1
Sophisticated	9	1.8
Enjoyed by women of stature–leisure–fame–wealth	7	1.4
Looks like platinum or white gold	6	1.2
Looks Italian–European	6	1.2
Looks custom designed	6	1.2
Top of the line	5	1.0
Authentic looking	5	1.0
Looks like real gold	4	0.8
Gourmet	4	0.8
Feel like a princess–queen–royalty	4	0.8
Tasteful	3	0.6
Total	498	100.0

DISCUSSION

In this article, I explored how issues of social class are manifested in the discourse of selling products to viewers through an analysis of home shopping television. From the results presented, it can be argued that home shopping programming addresses social class issues through the identification of financial limitations, the promise of status mobility through consumption, and anxiety provocation with regard to one's social standing. Of particular interest were comparisons of the discourse of Q2 versus QVC and HSN given the differences in the financial standing of their target audiences. What is systematically seen is that unlike QVC and HSN, Q2 did not spend a great deal of time selling class issues to its viewers. The following sections summarize the findings of this study with relation to the research questions posed in the beginning of this article.

Is There a Sales Discourse Identifying and Differentially Addressing Viewers' Social Class?

One goal of this research was to compare the discourse on Q2 with the two mainstream channels, QVC and HSN. It was theorized that if Q2 was marketing toward an upscale audience, a notable difference would be observed in the discourse. Indeed, on a number of levels I observed a difference between the rhetoric on Q2 and the rhetoric on QVC and HSN.

The Q2 channel and the QVC and HSN channels differed in other ways as well. For example, the product types for Q2 were markedly different. Q2 sold more electronics, home improvement items, office products, sporting goods, and exercise equipment. Clothing, cosmetics, and fashion accessories were not as popular on Q2. HSN and QVC, on the other hand, sold a majority of clothing, cosmetics, and fashion accessories. These more mainstream channels were low on the sale of electronics, home improvement products, office items, and exercise equipment. Thus, the Q2 audience was not targeted as much as the QVC and HSN audiences for sales of items involving image creation. It is likely less socially functional to sell image to an audience already holding a relatively more powerful social status.

Other significant differences regarding product type involved the jewelry offered for sale on the three channels. Ironically, Q2 sold the majority of synthetic stones, whereas QVC and HSN sold more authentic gemstones. This finding may make sense in light of the fact that wealthier viewers may not be purchasing their serious jewelry from home shopping channels. The synthetic jewels they purchase on home shopping may indeed constitute their fun jewelry, whereas for viewers of more modest means, the home shopping jewelry may in fact constitute their serious jewelry.

The pace of each sale was also markedly different among the three channels, with Q2 spending significantly less time on each product. For the Q2 audience, the less-is-more doctrine held true; saving time may be more relevant given that upscale viewers tend to spend less time watching television (Comstock, 1991; Comstock, Katzman, McCombs, & Roberts, 1978). It is therefore not surprising that the length of sale time is calibrated to parallel the viewing patterns of the targeted class.

For the majority of the sales discourse variables, HSN and QVC demonstrated similar patterns while differing from Q2. Rhetoric relating to financial prudence, upward mobility, trend setting, and trend following was present across the three channels but significantly higher for QVC and HSN. The fact that QVC had more in common with HSN than Q2 may seem surprising to those who are used to providing institutional analyses of media events. After all, much of the programming on Q2 was derived directly from QVC tapes. What is phenomenally important in this regard is the pattern of what was eliminated from QVC for subsequent airing on Q2. More specifically, Q2 programming was not merely a shortened version on routine

QVC material but rather a version that was shorter because many class issues pertinent to the projected QVC audience had been eliminated.

In considering variables related to financial prudence, the data on Q2 produced some differences worthy of discussion. In particular, the variables relating to getting the most for the money did not register as high for Q2 as they did for the other two channels. For example, Q2 offered the smallest percentage of items sold for versatility (e.g., a blouse that could be worn with either pants or a skirt, thus extending the number of ways it can be worn). Similarly, rhetoric regarding versatility of style (i.e., ability to be dressed up or down), versatility of color (i.e., items that match with anything), and versatility of season (i.e., those items that could be worn year-round) was significantly less common on Q2. Items were also said to be "affordable" less frequently on Q2. These findings all suggest that phrases relating to financial prudence and the financial limitations of viewers were not as important on the Q2 channel.

On Q2, the salespeople made far fewer references to items as classy or classic than on the other channels. In considering other variables in the upward-mobility category, Q2 also featured far fewer references to the elegance of an item. One possible explanation for this difference may be that Q2 sold relatively more technology and home furnishing and relatively less jewelry, clothing, and fashion accessories. It may be, then, that the former product types are less likely to invoke classy or classic epithets. However, in addition to the variation in product type, it is also likely that class-status terms were seen as less relevant to Q2 viewers. Conversely, upward-mobility terms are likely more common on QVC and HSN because these channels are appealing to an audience for whom upward social mobility is more of a dream.

To What Extent Can Home Shopping Discourse Generally be Interpreted As Economic Ideology?

The previous section demonstrated that differences exist among the home shopping channels with regard to issues of class. However, it is not simply that QVC and HSN are similar and Q2 was different. The significance is that these channels are different in an ideologically meaningful way. It is not so much what Q2 was doing but what the working-class shows are doing that was not prevalent on Q2.

To wit, as a genre of programming, home shopping is not merely a commercial vehicle that sells products but ideological acculturation with respect to both consumerism and social class. In all hierarchically ordered societies, the empowered are invariably outnumbered by the disempowered. As a result of this potentially dangerous imbalance, it is, arguably, necessary that the envy, discomfort, or hostility of the less affluent classes be contained so as to maintain the social order. In other words, the disempowered must adjust to their less advantaged positions. The storytelling, the rhetoric, the discourse of a culture, then, is often the major arena in which this adjustment is taught and in which social class adjustment is indoctrinated. The results of the study show that home shopping discourse can be seen as one such source of possible indoctrination. That is, a social adjustment function is at work.

As Thomas (1986) argued, other forms of mass media discourse (such as television sitcoms) may serve to quell class antagonisms by portraying vast possibilities for upward social mobility alongside grim and cynical portrayals of that mobility once achieved. Home shopping discourse operates in a similar manner on a conservative level, resolving the tensions between financial limitations and class aspirations. On the one hand, the discourse associates wealth with snobbery and pretension. On the other hand, it promises viewers an opportunity to achieve the look of wealth through consumption. Making purchases allows viewers to possess items that, according to the promise of home shopping, create the illusion of mobility. Ironically, the look of wealth is valued more highly than the condition itself. The items purchased through home shopping fulfill for buyers the class conditions they desire, providing an influence, however small, in maintaining social class structure.

Evidence of the promise of status mobility through consumption and the implied criticism of true wealth was a large part of the home shopping message. Viewers were repeatedly told when they were being offered something considered upscale. Depending on the cost of the product, however, wealth was either idealized or mocked. For example, a sales person pointed to the snobbery associated with wealth when trying to sell a less expensive item: "When you go to hoity toity high fashion stores … this is the kind of silver you see."[7] In other pitches, particularly for more expensive items, the rhetoric clearly emphasized the value of looking as if you have more than you do: "This looks like a one-of-a-kind, very high-end, very tailored jewelry item you had custom-designed for yourself."[8] In either case, conspicuous consumption is urged.

As a whole, financial prudence and upward mobility were very prevalent in the sales discourse of our home shopping programming. These results suggest that social class issues are central in the home shopping rhetoric. Financial limitations were clearly identified in the sales discourse, with the salespeople often positioning their products as providing the economically prudent alternative. As one host remarked during the sale of a beaded coin purse, "You don't have to go to debtor's prison for it."[9]

Many items were sold because they allegedly attracted attention. This aspect of the home shopping phenomenon is linked to the need to create an image. In the case of the synthetic stones and metals, the desired look is clearly that of someone who has a lot of money: "A bracelet like this in 18 karat gold would surely cost you over a thousand dollars. You'd be looking at $1,500 to $1,800 without a doubt. But you

---

[7]Jane Rudolph-Treacy, Quality–Value–Convenience, June 22, 1997.

[8]Lisa Mason, Quality–Value–Convenience, June 22, 1997.

[9]Kathy Levine, Quality–Value–Convenience, June 27, 1997.

know what? You get the best of both worlds today."[10] When the items for sale are more expensive, spending the money on the real thing is justified for the same reasons: "A bit more expensive, perhaps, but boy is it going to be worth it when you put that collection together. Heads will turn. And if you're buying something beautiful, you might as well go for the best."[11] Whether or not the item is expensive, the end goal is clear: Purchase the look of extravagance to impress others.

Rhetoric on following a trend was also prevalent on the home shopping channels. Interestingly, these types of terms were almost twice as common as the trend-setting terms, perhaps because offering something that is said to be fashionable or popular may allow the salespeople to position items as the key to status mobility. Nevertheless, fashion is still sold on a budget, with an emphasis on capturing a look of something bigger and better.

Haut couture, although sometimes mimicked on the home shopping programs, is positioned as unattainable. Claims by QVC that designs are copied from the high-fashion runways implies once again that achieving the look is just as satisfying as achieving the real thing. From a working-class standpoint, it is perhaps even more satisfying because it is obtained at a bargain price.

From the discussion of the research questions and results, it is clear that issues of social class play a role in the rhetoric of home shopping. The discourse on these programs promises viewers the illusion of status mobility through consumption. It also acknowledges financial limitations of viewers in an attempt to identify with viewers and relate to their financial situations. Finally, the rhetoric of home shopping programming encourages viewers to strive for an image. The goal for viewers, in home shopping terms, is to provide the illusion of wealth or to "look like a million bucks."[12]

CONCLUSIONS

Although this study provides evidence of the manner in which home shopping channels target class consciousness, a larger sample size may have yielded more data to strengthen some findings in this study. The frequencies for some terms under analysis were too small to yield significant statistical analyses. Therefore, expanding the sample size is desirable for further studies.

An additional limitation involved the time of year the sample was collected. The sample was drawn over a 2-week period during which there were no major holidays. It is possible that a holiday season may affect the products as well as the discourse, particularly with regard to the sale of children's items.

---

[10]Colleen Lopez, Home Shopping Network, June 26, 1997.
[11]Jane Rudolph-Treacy, Quality–Value–Convenience, June 25, 1997.
[12]Lisa Robertson, Quality–Value–Convenience, June 24, 1997.

Finally, the results of analyzing the discourse of home shopping programming may not be generalizable to other forms of advertising or programming. Home shopping is a unique hybrid of the two elements, and these findings represent only what one may find on other home shopping channels.

In this study, I have attempted to illuminate the discourse of home shopping programming. The perspective of the audience is still largely unknown. Audience analysis may provide valuable information with regard to how viewers respond to the sales discourse on the home shopping channels. Similarly, it may be useful to conduct interviews with the producers of home shopping programming.

Additionally, given that home shopping channels are not limited to the United States, further studies may attempt to compare the discourse of home shopping here with home shopping abroad. Asia, Europe, and Latin America offer home shopping channels, and it would be interesting to examine the cultural and ideological differences among the various channels.

Finally, further research may include a study of other interactive shopping methods such as Internet commerce. QVC already sells all its merchandise online at its Web site, earning more than a million dollars in sales during August 1997 (Balog, 1996). Similarly, HSN owns an online shopping venture called the Internet Shopping Network. Should televisions and computers continue to converge, shopping over the Internet may redefine what is meant by home shopping. This new form of shopping may have an interesting impact on the approach of the advertising industry to selling products to consumers.

In sum, I have attempted to illuminate how home shopping channels acknowledge the social class standings of their audiences. In an attempt to sell products, the channels reflect an awareness of economic limitations and express empathy for such limitations. By the same token, however, the sales discourse on home shopping may foster an anxiety over material conditions. This anxiety may be provoked by frequent references to the need to appear wealthy or classy. The home shopping sales discourse also suggests that viewers have a desire for upward mobility, a desire that, according to the sales discourse, can be satiated through consumption. Interestingly, the rhetoric only promises that viewers will achieve a look of the upper class; the actual mobility is not offered or even suggested as desired. In the world of home shopping, true class status does not matter, but its appearance is paramount. As a result, the salespeople encourage viewers to purchase home shopping ware to fulfill the look of the class condition they seek. Capitalism is promoted as the viewers become financially depleted and feed into the system. The purchases made may satisfy any desire for upward mobility, and thus quell class antagonisms.

Although evidence of social class awareness can be found on all three channels under analysis, many significant differences were noted with regard to the Q2 channel. If the Q2 channel were aimed at an upscale audience, as has been suggested, it appears that anxiety over social standing is not emphasized as powerfully for this market segment. Such findings allow us to speculate that home shopping programming keenly attends to the social status of its viewers.

ACKNOWLEDGMENT

This article could not have been possible without the help of Sari Thomas. Many thanks.

REFERENCES

Auter, P. J., & Moore, R. (1993). Buying from a friend: A content analysis of two teleshopping programs. *Journalism Quarterly, 70,* 425–436.

Balog, K. (1996, December 24). Online cybershoppers post record buying. *USA TODAY,* p. B1.

Berk, L. M. (1977). The great middle American dream machine. *Journal of Communication, 27*(3), 27–31.

Butsch, R. (1992). Class and gender in four decades of television situation comedy. *Critical Studies in Mass Communication, 9,* 387–399.

Butsch, R., & Glennon, L. (1980). Families on TV: Where was the working class? *Television, 7,* 10–12.

Comstock, G. (1991). *Television and the American child.* San Diego, CA: Academic.

Comstock, G., Katzman, N., McCombs, M., Roberts, D. (1978). *Television and human behavior.* New York: Columbia University Press.

Dobriner, W. M. (1963). *Class in suburbia.* Englewood Cliffs, NJ: Prentice-Hall.

Donaton, S. (1993, November 29). Home shopping audience widens. *Advertising Age,* 3.

Ewen, S. (1988). *All consuming images: The politics of style in contemporary culture.* New York: Basic.

Fallers, L. (1966). A note on the "trickle effect." In R. Bendix & S. Lipset (Eds.), *Class, status, and power* (pp. 402–405). New York: Free Press.

Gentile, F., & Miller, S. M. (1961). Television and social class. *Sociology and Social Research, 45,* 259–264.

Goldman, R. (1992). *Reading ads socially.* New York: Routledge.

Grant, A. E., Gutherie, K. K., & Ball-Rokeach, S. J. (1991). Television shopping: A media system dependency perspective. *Communication Research, 18,* 773–798.

Gumpert, G., & Drucker, S. (1992). From the agora to the electronic shopping mall. *Critical Studies in Mass Communication, 9,* 186–200.

Krippendorf, K. (1980). *Content analysis: An introduction to its methodology.* Beverly Hills, CA: Sage.

Landler, M. (1996, May 20). Diller to find new rivals as he updates old dream. *The New York Times,* p. D1 [Newspaper online]. Retrieved January 15, 1996 from the World Wide Web: http://search.nytimes.com/web/docsroot/library/cyber/week/0520barry.html

Laumann, E. (1966). *Prestige and association in an urban community.* New York: Bobbs-Merrill.

Leiss, W., Kline, S., & Jhally, S. (1990). *Social communication in advertising.* New York: Routledge.

Marchand, R. (1985). *Advertising the American dream: Making way for modernity, 1920–1940.* Los Angeles: University of California Press.

McAllister, M. P. (1996). *The commercialization of American culture.* Thousand Oaks, CA: Sage.

Petrozzello, D. (1998, August 31). Exit Q2, enter style. *Broadcasting & Cable, 128*(36), 72.

Packard, V. (1959). *The status seekers: An exploration of class behavior in America and the hidden barriers that affect you, your community, your future.* New York: McKay.

QVC. (1996, January). *Corporate facts* [Announcement posted on the World Wide Web]. Retrieved January 15, 1996 from the World Wide Web: http://www.qvc.com.hqfact.html

Thomas, S. (1986). Mass media and the social order. In G. Gumpert & R. Cathcart (Eds.), *Inter/Media: Interpersonal communication in a media world* (pp. 611–627). New York: Oxford University Press.

Thomas, S., & Callahan, B. (1982). Allocating happiness: TV families and social class. *Journal of Communication, 32*(3), 184–191.

Underwood, E. (1994). Queen of the superhighway: Carpenter takes QVC upscale. *Brandweek, 35*(4), 26–28.

Valdivia, A. (1997). The secret of my desire: Gender, class, and sexuality in lingerie catalogs. In K. Frith (Ed.), *Undressing the ad: Reading culture in advertising* (pp. 225–250). New York: Lang.

Veblen, T. (1899). *The theory of the leisure class*. New York: Macmillan.

Waldman, A. (1995, June). Lonely hearts, classy dreams, empty wallets. *The Washington Monthly, 27*(6), 10–16.

Warner, W., Meeker, M., & Eells, K. (1970). What social class is in America. In E. Laumann, P. Siegel, & R. Hodge (Eds.), *The logic of social hierarchies* (pp. 539–569). Chicago: Markham.

White, M. (1995). Watching the girls go buy: Shop-at-home television. In G. Dines & J. Humez (Eds.), *Gender, race and class in media* (pp. 152–159). Thousand Oaks, CA: Sage.

Zinn, L., De George, G., Shortez, R., Jones, D., & Anderson Forest, S. (1993, July 26). Retailing will never be the same. *Business Week*, 54–60.

MASS COMMUNICATION & SOCIETY, 2000, 3(4), 393–413

The Rise of Consumer Culture in a Chinese Society: A Reading of Banking Television Commercials in Hong Kong During the 1970s

Wendy Siuyi Wong

Department of Communication Studies
Hong Kong Baptist University

In this article, I analyze 2 case studies of television advertising campaigns for bank-
ing services during the 1970s and early 1980s in Hong Kong, those of Hang Seng
Bank and HongkongBank. Advertising from this period saw consumer society emerge
as traditional values and themes were adjusted to fit the imperatives of capitalism.
The earlier Hang Seng Bank campaign focused on the traditional banking practice of
saving, encouraging customers to work hard and gradually accumulate wealth. The
later HongkongBank campaign encouraged spending, immediate gratification of ma-
terial desires, and symbolic status achieved through acquisition of goods. As the case
studies show, this process entailed the reconfiguration of traditional Chinese values
to accommodate the arrival of consumerism in Hong Kong, a Chinese society.

The consumer society arises out of the ashes of traditional culture, which are characterized by relatively fixed forms for the satisfaction of needs .... The consumer society does not set up its own fixed models of behavior to replace traditional ones but
rather constructs, through marketing and advertising, successive waves of associations between persons, products, and images of well-being in an endless series of suggestions about the possible routes to happiness and success.

— Leiss, Kline, and Jhally (1990, p. 287)

Requests for reprints should be sent to Wendy Siuyi Wong, Department of Communication Studies,
Hong Kong Baptist University, Kowloon Tong, Kowloon, Hong Kong. E-mail: wsywong@yahoo.com

The functions of advertising have been understood from a number of theoretical perspectives, which range from a focus on the "justifiable goal" of providing consumers with information of "social value" (Sandage, 1972/1989, p. 6) to Marxist understandings that emphasize ideological functions such as the creation of a commodity-self and the promotion of a consumption-based society through advertising (Ewen, 1976). Examining two television advertising campaigns for the banking services of Hang Seng Bank (HSB) and HongkongBank (HKB) during the 1970s and early 1980s in Hong Kong, I show how economic and cultural shifts in Hong Kong were reflected at the discursive level. I argue that the development of consumer culture in Hong Kong required the modification of many traditional Chinese values. This article demonstrates how specific advertisements reflect changes toward values that integrate global trends in the banking business and are more amenable to consumerism. Because Hong Kong was the first Chinese society to experience a full and direct encounter with consumerism from the West, this study reveals the terms of the initial adjustment of Chinese values and ideals in response to consumer imperatives.

ADVERTISING DISCOURSE, CONSUMER CULTURE, AND SOCIAL CHANGE

The position here is between a strictly Marxist stance viewing advertising as a form of ideological and social control used by elites to manipulate the masses and a classical liberal position supporting the argument that advertising is a social good because "it is a proper and justifiable social goal to help consumers maximize their satisfaction" (Sandage, 1972/1989, p. 6). Critical scholars such as Ewen (1976) observed that to survive in a healthy form, capitalism must increase production and consumption, and advertising is arguably the fundamental means of doing this, through the "creation of desires and habits" (p. 37). Along these lines, Leiss et al. (1990) perceived that advertising functions to "appropriate and transform a vast range of symbols and ideas" (p. 5). Like their work, this article is based on the idea that advertising is a privileged discourse that appropriates, recirculates, and modifies cultural symbols.

This article focuses specifically on Hong Kong advertising as a means of exploring Hong Kong culture and history. It takes a cultural studies position, with advertising as the information system on which consumption is based (Slater, 1997) and that influences consumer needs and habits by conveying messages communicating meaning, values, and ideology. Bocock (1993) emphasized this role of advertising in furthering consumption:

> Modern consumerism ... depends upon its specific set of values becoming acceptable and comprehensible among sufficient groups of people so that sales of consumer

products can be made. These consumption-oriented values have to include those which either allow, or actively encourage, the purchase of the goods and experiences on offer. (p. 54)

The close textual analysis undertaken here reinforces the idea that the imperatives of advertising in terms of its ideological functions will be to a large extent the same no matter what culture, society, or country they are placed into. This study of the development of banking advertising provides an excellent example of this phenomenon. In its comparative examination of two banking advertisement campaigns, this article examines how the consumer society of Hong Kong arose "out of the ashes of traditional culture" (Leiss et al., 1990, p. 287), with traditional attitudes favoring personal sacrifice, hard work, and savings replaced or transformed into an emphasis on borrowing, consumption, and immediate gratification. This process can be seen as part of a larger process of globalization of consumer culture, founded on the insights that "people's attitudes about their finances are related to their education, and their values, not ... their nationalities" (Barnet & Cavanagh, 1994, p. 376) and that such attitudes can be influenced in any part of the world by advertising and expanded banking services that encourage spending and debt.

Barnet and Cavanagh (1994) offered a rich detailed history of the rise of information technology enabling financial transactions via global electronic networks and of the development of the multinational banking business with emphasis on the "financing of consumption rather than on the financing of production" (p. 383). With regard to this global trend toward the financing of consumption in terms of transfers through electronic data, credit cards, and debt in modern consumer society, scholars such as Baudrillard (1988), Bocock (1993), Lunt and Livingstone (1992), and Ritzer (1995) provided insightful ideological critiques. The close textual analysis undertaken here employs the ideas discussed in their works and examines the use of ideological themes and cultural values to convey images of desired behavior, the good life, and the goals and aspirations of individuals within society. The projection as found in the banking advertising of Hong Kong reflects not only the rise of consumer culture in a Chinese society but also the values and practices necessary in a global modern consumer society.

DEVELOPMENT OF HONG KONG SOCIETY, TELEVISION, AND ADVERTISING

Although Hong Kong was under British colonial rule from 1841 to 1997, it has always been a part of China geographically. As local sociologists Lau and Kuan (1988) observed, Hong Kong "still shares many of the same cultural characteristics" (p. 33) with China even today. However, it is "generally agreed among scholars and observers that ... the boundary between traditional and modern becomes blurred" (p. 3) in Hong Kong beginning in the late 1960s. At that time, "the divergence in the paths of development between Hong Kong and China intensified" (p. 1). Since the 1970s, Hong Kong has undergone rapid social change toward "an industrializing, modernizing and predominantly urban society exposed to Western acculturation and immersed in cosmopolitanism" (p. 33).

Three strands of development in Hong Kong worked together to make the 1970s a key decade of growth toward consumer society. This decade saw rapid changes in levels of production, in increased wages, and in the spread of television to virtually all Hong Kong households (Leung, 1996). The flourishing of advertising cannot occur without the industrialization of a society, as the cases in Great Britain and the United States illustrate (see Lears, 1994; Marchand, 1985; Richards, 1990). As Sze (1997) pointed out, the popularity of Hong Kong television began with the establishment in November 1967 of Hong Kong Television Broadcasts (TVB), the first wireless television station in Hong Kong. By 1968, the home penetration rate reached 12.3%; by 1971, 60.6%; by 1975, 88.8% (Hong Kong Television Advisory Board, 1967–1987). With this background, the television commercials throughout the 1970s are well positioned to reflect and project the changes of the society as the traditional culture interacted with the newly evolving values.

According to Yiu's (1997) classification of the important developmental stages of the Hong Kong economy, the period of industrial growth and diversification in Hong Kong lasted from 1960 through 1979 and was followed by a period of industrial transformation in the post-1980 era. During the period from the 1970s through the 1980s, when the banking advertisements analyzed here were produced, Hong Kong was rapidly becoming an affluent, fully developed capitalist society. Television advertising in Hong Kong thus became dominant as the society completed its growth and diversification stage and remained dominant through the industrial transformation stage.

The success of Hong Kong in moving rapidly through the stages of economic development to a stage of relative affluence also provided the population with some disposable income and further contributed to the health of the advertising industry by providing a large percentage of workers with adequate means for consumption. Leung (1996) referred to the period following the mid-1970s as one of structural change, marked by "the increasing affluence of the community, the rising educational attainment of the population, and the expansion of the financial and service sectors" (p. 11). These changes brought about the "birth of a new middle class" (p. 12), which had a different set of attitudes and social aspirations and a different lifestyle from manual laborers. With these developments in the economy, television availability, and the rise of the middle class, the 1970s and early 1980s saw the alteration and replacement of traditional Chinese values in Hong Kong and their recombination with Western attitudes toward consumption (Leung, 1996), a process that can clearly be seen through comparative examination of the two banking campaigns during this period.

SELECTION OF THE CASE STUDIES

This study of banking advertisements of HSB and HKB provides an excellent illustration of how traditional values change toward those more amenable to consumerism. The two selected case studies show that traditional Chinese values in financial practice that did not conform to the "organic necessities" (Sinclair, 1987, p. 24) of advertising within the capitalist system were reconfigured as Hong Kong developed into an advanced capitalist economy. It is easy to see how the traditional Chinese value of saving money directly contradicts the capitalist imperative of spending and acquisition as the signs of wealth and success. Television advertising is one of the most powerful media to provoke the desire of the audience and encourage habits of consumption and gratification that are in effect the opposite of the traditional Chinese way of thinking, which emphasized self-denial and self-sacrifice as the means of saving money and acquiring increasing wealth.

The two case studies examined here illustrate two quite distinct strategies based on two different sets of values and ideals. The first campaign, that of HSB, ran throughout the 1970s and was accompanied by corporate sponsorship of educational programs in elementary schools to further establish a corporate identity tied heavily to the Chinese community in Hong Kong. By the 1980s, both the educational programs and highly visible thematic television advertising campaigns of HSB had virtually disappeared. On the other hand, whereas earlier HKB ads such as "Cartoon Lion" (1972) and "Vicky Wong" (1975) were simple and direct, they did not make references to social values, either traditional or consumerist. In the 1980s, HKB began to turn more toward new consumerist values within their advertisements, focusing on technological innovations and changes in banking services and products. The HKB ads for new services and technologies incorporated values incompatible with traditional Chinese attitudes toward saving, whereas HSB television advertising all but disappeared from view. Thus, although some of the difference between the strategies observed here can be attributed to the different corporate images and brand identities of the two banks, the focus of argument is on the historical shift of values required by the encroachment of consumerism into Hong Kong society. In fact, there are no ongoing television banking campaigns after the 1970s that incorporate traditional Chinese values as did the HSB ads of the 1970s.

All the advertisements analyzed in this article were taken from the commercial historical archives of these two banks. HKB archivists kept a complete set of their advertisements throughout the period under examination. HSB records of advertising campaigns were less well kept, and information on production dates was in some cases estimated based on *Hang Seng: The Evergrowing Bank* (Chambers,

1991). Although the set of advertisements analyzed may not be complete, it is certainly representative of the style and themes taken up by the bank at the time. Because so many ads made up each campaign and space does not allow close examination of each ad, sample advertisements representative of the whole were chosen for close analysis. In addition, brief informational ads that plainly describe products and services were not selected for close analysis.

Although the shift of values as reflected in the campaigns of both banks is at least in small part due to the different advertising strategies of the two banks, the appearance of the 1980s HKB campaigns also reflected the society that was emerging in Hong Kong at that time. Thus, this chronological juxtaposition of the HSB campaign of the 1970s and the HKB campaign starting in the 1980s is perfectly situated historically to illustrate the rapidity and thoroughness of the cultural change under discussion. The examination of these campaigns provides clear evidence that the development of modern methods in the banking industry, along with the emergence of consumer culture, required the rejection of traditional Chinese values, which were rapidly replaced by Western-derived notions of acceptable practices, honorable behavior, and the good life according to the messages underlying those campaigns. Values shifted from a focus on savings to encouraging borrowing, from self-reliance to reliance on bank loans, from hard work to easy spending, from real to symbolic status, and from harmony with nature to focus on material goods.

HSB: EDUCATING THE EXCELLENT VIRTUE OF SAVING

The name *Hang Seng Bank* in Cantonese means "ever-growing bank," and the history of the development of the company has followed the name. The bank was originally founded as Hang Seng Ngan Ho by S. H. Ho and three business partners in 1933. Under the leadership and influence of Ho, the philosophy of the bank upheld traditional Chinese values throughout the 1970s. The advertising strategy of HSB thus relied on references to Chinese philosophical elements such as the importance of knowledge and experience and the value of hard work. Under Ho's leadership, by the end of the 1970s, HSB was the second-largest bank in Hong Kong, with only HKB larger (Chambers, 1991). The bank was important to the development of Chinese businesses and worked primarily with Chinese people as Hong Kong grew into an industrialized society. Compared to other non-Chinese banks such as HKB, HSB represented a reputable and stable banking outlet where Chinese customers felt comfortable because both bank and customers shared common traditional Chinese values. Throughout the early decades of the life of the bank, the philosophy of giving something back to the society was reflected through the charity actions and advertisements of HSB that emphasized hard work and close-knit community as the means to achieve a better life.

The Virtue of Saving

Throughout the television ads of HSB, references to Chinese values, philosophical issues, practices of life, and Confucianism were included as the primary elements of persuasive appeal. For example, one ad used the occasion of Chinese New Year (CNY) to present its central character and spokesperson as the God of Fortune (see Figure 1). The God of Fortune greeted viewers with a five-character poem wishing people a happy and prosperous new year. The poem represented a traditional type of Chinese life practice and translates as "practice saving in the teenage years, work energetically when you are still young, then in your middle life you will get everything for your life, and in old age you will have a happy family life." The key message of the ad apart from the simple and literal greeting for CNY reflected some of the principles of HSB at that time. The merit and practices directed to viewers were those found in Chinese traditional thinking and values. As Feng (1988) summarized, "Chinese traditional values include not only Confucian social ethical values, but also Taoistic natural ethical values" (p. 58). Social ethical values can include "love of one's fellow men [and] honesty" (p. 58), and natural ethical values can refer to "self-regulation, self-enrichment, [and] self-prudence" (p. 58). Clearly, the ad preached to the audience on the righteousness of Chinese traditional values of "self with other, with society, and with nature" (p. 58). These values were linked abstractly with the security of savings, such that money represented peace and sta-

FIGURE 1   God of Fortune, Hang Seng Bank, 1973.

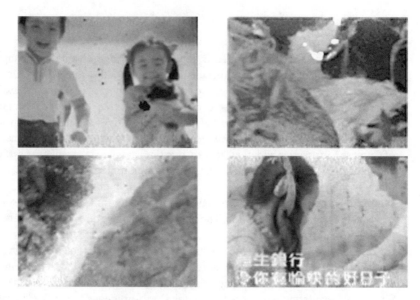

FIGURE 2   Little Water Drop, Hang Seng Bank, 1972.

bility rather than the elements of choice, leisure, and purchasing power that were emphasized in the later HKB campaign.

Two additional HSB ads from the 1970s illustrate the emphasis the bank placed on savings as a personal practice connected with the broader traditional Chinese values just described. One of their very early ads, Little Water Drop (see Figure 2), produced around 1972, illustrated the virtue of saving by using metaphor accompanied by a musical jingle. The jingle included the line "even a little water drop can gather into an ocean. Even a grain of sand can build the land." The visual provided a match for the jingle, opening with three young children chasing their puppy on the beach and flying a kite. The visual cut to an image of a drop of water while the jingle was about the little water drop. The water drop was superimposed onto a visual of a big waterfall, and the waterfall cut to the ocean, providing the literal visual representation of the jingle lyrics. Next, some floating sand was shown, and it formed a pile that became a piece of land. The images of the ocean and the land were intercut with each other, and then the visual returned to the children playing in the sand. Finally, the male voice-over stated that "accumulation from very small can become very great. Hang Seng Bank can arrange a happy life for you."

Sand in the ad is not only a metaphor for savings but also a familiar plaything that may invoke fond memories or hopes of future fun times. As Lunt and Livingstone (1992) noted, "attitudes to finances reflect more general underlying values which guide people's attitudes and behaviours in many life domains" (p. 119). As can be seen in this ad, the emphasis was on dependable growth from a small amount to an exaggerated large amount (a whole ocean), suggesting that full success and happiness can be found through the simple practice of saving. This traditional attitude toward money and the personal financial practices that will bring success, as well as the type of success that is depicted, are in clear contrast to later banking ads in Hong Kong. Not only did the HSB ad focus on traditional values and practices connected with money, it also depicted success as simple enjoyment of life unrelated to consumption of goods. The kite, an item that can be purchased for a very small price or even made by hand, was the only consumer item that appeared in the ad. The children played together in a natural setting, enjoying each other and natural elements, and they used their imagination and energy to create fun.

The Value of Hard Work

An ad produced for the 40th anniversary of the HSB (see Figure 3) in 1973 drew on the same themes used in the earlier ads but placed even more emphasis on the idea of working with Hong Kong people to ensure a better future through mutual efforts. This ad included many images of building construction in the city, on the harbor, and so forth, generally giving the impression of the hustle and bustle of the society as it progressed into its more modernized form. The streets were filled with vehicles, airplanes flew overhead, and ships sailed through the harbor. These images were contrasted with images of a farmer plowing land with a single ox. The contrast

FIGURE 3   Hang Seng Bank 40th Anniversary, 1973.

implied that society had developed quite far from the old farming method to the more modern symbols of high-rise buildings and airplanes. However, it also seemed to suggest that the farmer provides both nourishment and a solid past on which the development is based. The visuals are somewhat open to interpretation as to the position and meaning of the farmer in relation to the modern city, but the verbal text provided the anchor for these floating signifiers. It said, "energetic Hong Kong, progressive Hong Kong, it all depends on cultivation and hard work."

The second part of the ad again depicted the farmer working with the ox, plowing a row for planting. This visual was intercut with an image of a paved road. The camera kept moving forward, making the road pass quickly under the viewer's eyes. Meanwhile, the background music was fast paced and enhanced the feeling of forward movement. Subtitles read "with cultivation, with harvest, with hard work, with future." The ad closed with the moving road image again, along with the HSB logo. Thus, progress and future were re-emphasized as the central themes of the ad but were connected with traditional values. As a whole, the ad conveyed the idea that if people work hard, they can have a good future, just as Hong Kong as a society did in moving from simple farming techniques to an industrialized and modern city in just a short time. The bank subtly associated itself with the progress that Hong Kong made toward a happy, prosperous future but again did not mention material goods that can be obtained with money, or any of its services, advantages over competitors, and so forth.

Whereas the 40th anniversary ad just described conveyed a general message about hard work applicable to the whole society of Hong Kong, a later example took a much more personal approach. This ad focused on a blue-collar worker (see Figure 4) telling his story in images without voice-over narration. The story started with a man working on a pier unloading stock from boats. He passed a truck in which the driver was taking a rest in the cab and seemed to envy the truck driver. The following scene showed a group of pier workers gathered together and gambling for fun. The visual zoomed away to the central protagonist, who was eating lunch alone. He took out his HSB passbook and smiled in satisfaction. Then, the visual cut to the next scene, which showed a new truck with the young man inside. His friend congratulated him on having his own truck. Next, he was shown delivering goods and then instructing workers. Instead of wearing the simple t-shirt he had been wearing, he was wearing a work shirt with buttons and pockets. He inspected a row of trucks, and his former colleague cleaned them and called him "boss." The visual ended with a shot of him inspecting the trucks, and a male voice-over provided the only anchoring words in the ad: "It is not just luck to be a success. It is about hard work and ability." This ad illustrated and praised the value of hard work and promoted the traditional belief that if you work hard you can achieve success in life. Success is defined purely as position rather than as the purchase of goods or enjoyment of leisure time. The content of this ad and the others reflects a production-based rather than a consumption-based society and reflects the traditional val-

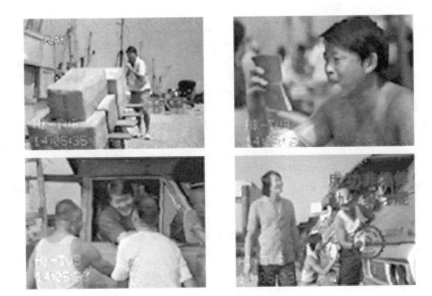

FIGURE 4   Truck Driver, Hang Seng Bank, 1979.

ues of self-reliance, hard work, harmonious family and society, and gradual accumulation toward security and position.

As Ritzer (1995) pointed out, banks traditionally tried to get people to be debt-free and to engage in the practice of saving. The HSB ads in this direction could easily follow both the banking tradition and the tradition of Chinese values because they were together in their concept that hard work and saving were the correct path to wealth and happiness. This theme of saving and hard work in the HSB ads continued through the mid-1970s. The ads used very similar techniques by linking the idea of saving and hard work with the idea of happiness and personal satisfaction, without any reference to consumer goods or the ideas and practices of consumption. They also subtly conveyed the idea of harmony between people and nature. Happiness was depicted as simple enjoyment of family members or friends in a peaceful or familiar setting. There was no reference at all to what the accumulated money could buy in the material sense. The only "good" depicted was the enjoyment of a simple life in harmony with nature. The attitude toward the importance of hard work and the link between saving and future happiness were easily connected through the traditional values referenced in the ads.

HKB: PROMOTING THE PLEASURE OF BORROWING

The Hongkong and Shanghai Banking Corporation's HongkongBank (HKB) was founded in 1865 by a group of British and foreign businessmen in Hong Kong shortly after the end of the Second Sino–British War (King, 1991). The name in Chinese, *Wayfoong,* means in the literal sense "a focus on wealth." It was the sole British overseas bank that had its headquarters in Hong Kong, and by 1900 it had become the dominant local bank as well as very powerful in China. As a sort of central bank, which produces most of the local currency, it serves as the main bank of the Hong Kong government. Unlike HSB, HKB does not have any special commitment toward the Hong Kong Chinese community but rather distinguishes itself as a British-owned bank (King, 1991). The HKB campaigns project a more Westernized image and focus more on the commercial purposes, services, and values related to consumption. Their early 1980s campaigns picked up the technological development, diversification of banking services, and economic transformation of Hong Kong society, providing a clear contrast with the HSB campaigns described previously. This campaign was moving toward an emphasis on symbolic status achieved through material goods rather than actual achievement and position gained through hard work, as in HSB campaigns.

Spending with Convenient Cash

In the electronic teller counter (ETC) campaign, the elements of ease and convenience were emphasized regularly. ETC provided a computerized machine teller that could be utilized at any time of day or night to withdraw or deposit money. This campaign introduced the newly available service in 1980. Because ETC was a new service, the ads focused on what it was, how to apply for it, and what it provided to the user. Sword Man (see Figure 5) depicted a character taken from a popular television epic at the time, performed by Cheng Siu-tsau. The ad first stated the problem that sometimes a person needs money at an awkward time when the bank is closed. The setting was at night outside one of the bank branches where the television character was attacked by several people. He pulled out the ETC card, put it into the bank machine slot, and punched his code number with one hand while defending himself from the attackers with the other. When the money appeared, he addressed the audience, saying, "so easy you can do it with one hand." From this very first ETC ad, the emphasis was on withdrawal rather than deposit of funds. The service itself leads to a more casual attitude toward spending, as it eliminates the need to plan how much money to keep on hand for likely expenditures, and the ad pushed the consumer even further in this direction, indicating that the card is "just like money in your pocket" and removing the connection between work and money as well as the connection between what you put into the account and what you can take out. The emphasis on ease and convenience carries with it a lack of concern for how much money is spent and with what frequency.

Another ad from the same campaign, Amah (Chinese domestic helper), more literally made the connection between the convenience of the machine and spending. This ad (see Figure 6) depicted an Amah with the male voice-over saying that some-

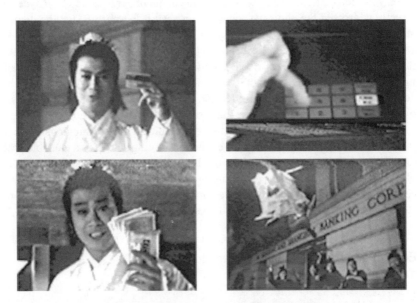

FIGURE 5   Sword Man, HongkongBank, 1980.

FIGURE 6   Amah, HongkongBank, 1980.

times you need cash for a holiday. The Amah got out of her boss's Rolls Royce and directly addressed the audience, saying how easy it is to use ETC. She demonstrated using the card to get cash, saying "now you can have cash seven days a week. Otherwise, how could I get enough to spend?" Thus the ad emphasized that the function of the machine is to make withdrawal more convenient and potentially more frequent. The deposit function was not mentioned in this or any of the other ads in the introductory campaign. Rather, convenience was mentioned over and over, and ETC was linked with the ideas of instant cash and spending money.

Unlike the HSB commercials discussed previously, these campaigns made no mention of hard work and certainly were not promoting saving as a valuable practice. The virtues of saving and hard work have disappeared in these HKB ads, replaced by a new set of values emerging in the procredit era. These new values of consumption and easy spending were further developed and emphasized in the HKB campaigns for VISA® Card and personal installment loans (PIL).

Encouragement of Casual Consumption Through the Credit Card

As Ritzer (1995) pointed out, the credit card is now an American icon that "is treasured, even worshipped, in the United States and, increasingly throughout the rest of the world" (p. 1). Because much of the consumption and lifestyle development in the society of Hong Kong has followed the experience of the West (Leung, 1996), the credit card phenomenon eventually evolved in Hong Kong, and the early 1980s proved to be the most important phase in the development into the credit era. Following Simmel's (1907/1990) notion of the philosophy of money, Ritzer (1995) defined the function of credit cards as "permit[ting] people to spend more than they have" (p. 3). Indeed, even in the television advertisements from the first launch of the credit card in Hong Kong, such a depiction of casual consumption images can be commonly found. Naturally, this new development represented a clear move away from the traditional values depicted in the earlier HSB campaigns because "the credit card is yet another invention of the banks and other financial institutions to get people to save less and spend more" (Ritzer, 1995, p. 10).

The HKB VISA® Card campaign introduced credit cards available from the bank. Its first ad, launched in 1980 (see Figure 7), opened with the visual display of the VISA® Card with a narrator saying that "this is a VISA® Card, but not just any VISA® Card. It is VISA® from HongkongBank. The international VISA® Card that lets you make the important purchase when you need to." The visual display of the VISA® Card presented the card as a sign of consumption. The credit card became a sign of purchasing power and convenience that allows for consumption without cash notes and even without savings in the bank. The consumption activities depicted in the ad included using the card to pay for dinner in a fancy restaurant

FIGURE 7   Launch of Visa® Card, HongkongBank, 1980.

and using it to purchase household electronic appliances, clear signs of affluence for the emerging middle class in Hong Kong.

The follow-up ad in the same year, Suit (see Figure 8), depicted more purchasing scenarios. The narrative mentioned that this card can make any purchase so much easier and simpler, including "things you have to buy" and "things you want to buy" and even "the things you really do not intend to buy." In this ad the things you have to buy were represented by household electronic appliances, the things you want to buy were represented by a fancy hat for a woman, and the things you do not intend to buy were represented by a toy. In the restaurant scene, the man hardly looked at the bill but immediately put out his credit card to pay. The card was accepted happily by the waiter, whose attitude further confirmed the status of the user. This ad presented the credit card not only as a sign of status but also as a trouble-free means of acquisition in a variety of circumstances.

In Baudrillard's (1988) terms, this "most modern form of payment, [that seemingly can] free us from checks, cash, and even from financial difficulties at the end of the month" (p. 34) easily lends itself to such a trouble-free representation. As Ritzer (1995) pointed out, credit cards can "smooth out consumption by allowing us to make purchases even when our incomes are low" (p. 4). These introductory ads depicted the advantages and convenience of the card, which allows the purchase of such unnecessary items as a fancy restaurant meal and a pretty hat. As Baudrillard stated, "in order to become an object of consumption, the object must

FIGURE 8   Suit, HongkongBank, 1980.

become a sign" (p. 22). The objects became signs of power, happiness, and status. The status of position represented in the HSB ads was progressively replaced by the symbolic status of credit and purchasing power. The VISA® ads took the first step in this process.

Ritzer (1995) warned about the hidden dangers of credit cards, observing that although "credit cards seem to be the means to wealth, happiness, and liberation from our otherwise humdrum lives" (p. 11), they actually end up serving as "instruments of bondage locking people into a lifetime of indebtedness" (p. 11). As can be seen from the VISA® Card ads from HKB, although a line such as "the things you really do not intend to buy" may be intended as humorous, it is also an illustration of how the card can manipulate demand. Also, by displaying different cases and problems (e.g., from having to buy electronic appliances to wanting to buy a hat) followed by the solution of the card, the ads illustrate what Baudrillard (1988) criticized in noting that "everything is appropriated and simplified into the translucence of abstract 'happiness,' simply defined by the resolution of tensions" (p. 34). The images of these ads provided an easy solution to the viewers and projected a kind of satisfactory and happy picture that they could obtain by owning the card. The main reason is that "the money involved in credit card transactions seems abstract and unreal" (Ritzer, 1995, p. 60). Clearly the HKB ads enhanced this effect by eliminating references to work, accumulation, and gradual growth toward security and status, elements fundamental to the traditional Chinese value system that were still present in the HSB ads of the late 1970s.

Although the ads did not overtly state that debt is good, they promoted associations between credit cards and material consumption that more subtly encourage debt-producing behaviors. The move into the realm of buying things that are unnecessary and not desirable and purchasing things that are not at all considered ahead of time placed additional focus on consumption in connection with satisfaction and enjoyment of life. Thus, the HKB VISA® Card campaign took another step toward the values of consumption and lifestyle and away from traditional values of self-reliance, hard work, and saving. Although the element of debt lies unspoken behind the mechanism of a credit card, it is not an explicit requirement of a life of consumption. This step was not taken until the PIL was introduced in 1983.

The Enjoyments of Loans

In Hong Kong, as elsewhere, modernization has meant a significant shift in the purposes, goals, and techniques of banking and bank advertising, such that today "while banks are discouraging savings, they are in various ways encouraging debt" (Ritzer, 1995, p. 10). Whereas the VISA® Card uses the idea of credit to encourage consumption, the PIL makes debt a way of further enhancing the possibilities of gratification through material goods. This debt concept is contradictory to traditional Chinese thinking, bringing the values espoused in the HKB ads in clear opposition to those values emphasized in the earlier HSB campaigns. Debt is not only clearly contrary to traditional Chinese values but also a concept imported from the West. As Lunt and Livingstone (1992) observed, in the West people believe that "debt is a normal part of everyday life and nothing to be ashamed of" (p. 119). Therefore, in depicting the use of the PIL for a wide variety of everyday and extravagant expenses, the ads served as a legitimization of the practice already made acceptable in the West, showing debt as something acceptable, right, normal, or even preferred rather than presenting the traditional Chinese view of debt as shameful.

The PIL ads focused not on the specifics of how to take out a loan but rather on how the bank was acting like a friend by helping the customer. The ad (see Figure 9) that launched this campaign, entitled, Thank You HongkongBank (1983), opened with the scene of the harbor view from the peak. A couple was depicted watching the sunset over the harbor and discussing something, with the conclusion, "let's ask HongkongBank," just as a person may say, "let's ask our friend." The second scene showed another couple in an electronics store. They were short of money to purchase the household appliances they wanted and said they would talk to HongkongBank. Finally, a third scene showed another young couple standing in front of the window display of a travel agency. The visual cut to the inside of a bank with a poster advertising the PIL. Again the visual cut to show the results of the problems of the three couples depicted earlier. The couple who was watching the sunset was at their wedding banquet, the electronics store couple was sitting in their

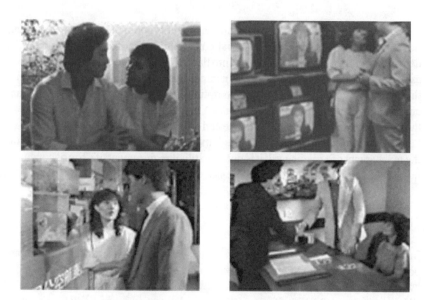

FIGURE 9   Thank You HongkongBank, 1983.

living room watching a new television, and the travel agency couple was in front of a check-in counter at the airport. All of them said, "Thank you HongkongBank."

Advertisements help in "constructing consumers' sense of themselves as composed by particular kinds of product-images" (Goldman, 1992, p. 34), and these PIL ads helped consumers imagine themselves in new situations brought about by the consumption of goods made possible through a loan. Thus, the ads sold not only the idea of a loan but also images of lifestyles and identities made possible by consumption. The young couples desired consumer goods as the route to happiness, yet they did not seem to work for these goods. Instead, their desires were immediately gratified through the acquisition of debt. Again the elements of actual money, true costs, work, and savings were eliminated from view. A happy life was depicted as one that includes quick purchase of goods to fulfill material desires rather than one that builds slowly toward a stable and secure lifestyle.

With the simple technique of showing a series of desires linked up with the ability of the bank to help obtain these desires immediately, before the hard work has been done to earn them, these ads implied that debt is a good way to solve problems. The shift here is more significant than simply encouraging the sale of a particular service and more important than simply selling the idea of a new image of life and lifestyle. In fact, the shift from the earlier emphasis on savings to the final stage of the PIL ads involved a fundamental replacement of values. This shift was necessary to the successful functioning of industrial capitalism and was thus inevitable as the economy of Hong Kong developed. The comparison of these two bank case studies, with the later one used to sell a range of new technologically innovative services, shows a dramatic shift in values and desires projected within a very small time frame. Whereas the earlier HSB ads were free of consumer goods, the HKB campaigns showed a wide range of goods, lifestyle images, and materially solvable problems to help instill desires and encourage consumption. With the easy money provided by loans, consumers' dreams can come true, and the practical value of the products in terms of money and labor is no longer an issue to be considered.

Thus, through the projection of visual depiction of the ad at the symbolic level, the PIL ads from HKB at this time reflected the society of Hong Kong as evolving toward the modern capitalism stage. According to Bocock (1993), many societies have a large proportion of those

> Who increasingly are hooked into the culture of consumerism. This means that many people continue to desire to be purchasers, consumers, even when they cannot afford to buy all the things and pleasurable experiences which they might wish as a consequence of seeing what is on offer in advertisements, and in television programmes more generally. (p. 76)

By depicting debt as a normal activity that is acceptable in nearly any situation where a large expenditure is needed or desired, the HKB ads definitely contributed to this phenomenon that is characteristic of "Western capitalist social formations" (Bocock, 1993, p. 76). Of course, the ads did not mention interest rates or fees, the terms or methods of repayment, or the amount of money to be borrowed. They simply took consumption for granted and invited consumption with money not yet earned. The introduction of the VISA® Card and the PIL represents the development of Hong Kong toward a consumption-based society. To be modern is not just to be surrounded by goods but also to utilize modern practices and habits of consumption as originally developed in the West, such that "the consumer goods and experiences do deliver, for some, the goal of life-consuming things" (Bocock, 1993, p. 51), in Hong Kong as in the West. Not only are people no longer encouraged to save, but they are encouraged to go into debt to pay for the symbols of modern life. Therefore, debt in its various forms, including credit cards and bank loans, becomes one of the necessities of modern life. To encourage debt, the ads must alter traditional values, placing self-reliance and work in the background and presenting goods and spending as the way to achieve happiness.

CONCLUSIONS

This article has provided a comparative case study to illustrate how "consumerism has become the practical ideology of capitalism, one which legitimates capitalism in the daily lives and everyday practices of millions of inhabitants of western, and other, social formations" (Bocock, 1993, p. 116). In doing so, consumerism reconfigures the traditional values of a society with values required by capitalism and consumption. Examples from the Hong Kong cases illustrate this phenomenon. This analysis has shown not only that the development of capitalism requires the abandonment or alteration of traditional values but also that the process of modernization in Hong Kong was a process of Westernization, through which values and ideals developed in the West were imported to carry out the imperatives of consumer capitalism. In Hong Kong, modern consumer culture truly arose from the ashes of traditional culture, bringing with it a change not only in habits of consumption but also in fundamental cultural values and ideals. In examining these relations, this article has explicated the ideological functions and meanings of advertising that contributed to the fertilization and sustenance of the life of the capitalist system in Hong Kong.

ACKNOWLEDGMENTS

I thank Hank Seng Bank and HongkongBank for providing tapes of their archived advertisements. I am grateful for the detailed and considerate attention given to the article by editors Sharon Mazzarella and Matthew McAllister. Thanks also to my dissertation supervisor, Dr. Jackie Kwok at the Hong Kong Polytechnic University.

REFERENCES

Barnet, R. J., & Cavanagh, J. (1994). *Global dreams: Imperial corporations and the new world order.* New York: Simon & Schuster.
Baudrillard, J. (1988). *Jean Baudrillard: Selected writings* (M. Poster, Trans.). Oxford, England: Polity.
Bocock, R. (1993). *Consumption.* New York: Routledge.
Chambers, G. (1991). *Hang Seng: The evergrowing bank.* Hong Kong: Heng Seng Bank.
Ewen, S. (1976). *Captains of consciousness: Advertising and the social roots of the consumer culture.* New York: McGraw-Hill.
Feng, L. (1988). Chinese modernisation and social values. In D. Sinha & H. S. R. Kao (Eds.), *Social values and development: Asian perspectives* (pp. 56–64). Newbury Park, CA: Sage.
Goldman, R. (1992). *Reading ads socially.* New York: Routledge.
Hong Kong Television Advisory Board. (1967–1987). *Report of the Television Advisory Board on the progress of television in Hong Kong* (Vols. 1–12). Hong Kong: Government Printer.
King, F. H. H. (1991). *The history of the Hongkong and Shanghai Banking Corporation* (Vol. 4). Hong Kong: Hongkong and Shanghai Banking Corporation.
Lau, S. K., & Kuan, H. C. (1988). *The ethos of the Hong Kong Chinese.* Hong Kong: Chinese University Press.
Lears, J. (1994). *Fables of abundance: A cultural history of advertising in America.* New York: Basic.
Leiss, W., Kline, S., & Jhally, S. (1990). *Social communication in advertising: Persons, products and images of well-being* (2nd ed.). New York: Routledge.
Leung, B. K. P. (1996). *Perspectives on Hong Kong society.* Hong Kong: Oxford University Press.

Lunt, P. K., & Livingstone, S. M. (1992). *Mass consumption and personal identity: Everyday economic experience.* Philadelphia: Open University Press.

Marchand, R. (1985). *Advertising the American dream: Making way for modernity, 1920–1940.* Berkeley: University of California Press.

Richards, T. (1990). *The commodity culture of Victorian England: Advertising and spectacle, 1815–1914.* New York: Verso.

Ritzer, G. (1995). *Expressing America: A critique of the global credit card society.* Thousand Oaks, CA: Pine Forge.

Sandage, C. H. (1989). Some institutional aspects of advertising. In R. Hovland & G. B. Wilcox (Eds.), *Advertising in society: Classic and contemporary readings on advertising's role in society* (pp. 3–10). Lincolnwood, IL: NTC Business Books. (Original work published 1972)

Simmel, G. (1990). *The philosophy of money* (2nd ed.). New York: Routledge. (Original work published 1907)

Sinclair, J. (1987). *Images incorporated: Advertising as industry and ideology.* New York: Routledge.

Slater, D. (1997). *Consumer culture and modernity.* Cambridge, England: Polity.

Sze, M. H. (1997). Mass culture and consumption life [In Chinese]. In K. M. Wang (Ed.), *Hong Kong history: New perspectives* (Vol. 2, pp. 593–615). Hong Kong: Joint Publishing.

Yiu, M. K. (1997). The history of industrial development in Hong Kong [In Chinese]. In K. M. Wang (Ed.), *Hong Kong history: New perspectives* (Vol. 1, pp. 371–416). Hong Kong: Joint Publishing.

MASS COMMUNICATION & SOCIETY, 2000, 3(4), 415–437

Encoding Advertisements: Ideology and Meaning in Advertising Production

Matthew Soar

Department of Communication
University of Massachusetts, Amherst

In this article I argue for the expansion of cultural studies to include sustained research into the subjective aspects of commercial cultural production. In particular, I focus on an analysis of creative workers in advertising and design, presenting historical notes, theoretical elaboration, and empirical evidence to explore the social stratum Bourdieu (1984) identified as the "new cultural intermediaries" (p. 366). It is argued that the first—and often the only—audience ad creatives and designers have in mind is themselves; furthermore, this work is in itself a form of cultural sustenance. An underlying commitment here is that cultural studies should expand beyond its investigations of consumption, the text, and reception. A schematic model is proposed that takes an existing conception of the project of cultural studies and adapts it to the findings presented herein.

Obviously people invent and produce adverts, but apart from the fact that they are unknown and faceless, the ad in any case does not claim to speak for them, it is not their speech.

—Williamson (1978, p. 14)

Stripping away the veil of anonymity and mystery would by itself be of great value in demystifying the images that parade before our lives and through which we conceptualize the world and our role within it.

—Jhally (1995, p. 86)

These quotations are indicative of two opposing and apparently incompatible views about how to assess the cultural and political import of advertising. Whereas

Requests for reprints should be sent to Matthew Soar, Department of Communication, University of Massachusetts, Amherst, Machmer Hall, Box 34815, Amherst, MA 01003–4815. E-mail: soar@comm.umass.edu

Jhally (1995) advocated a line of inquiry that includes the production of "image-based culture" (p. 77), Williamson's (1978) influential argument is founded on the assertion that this is a futile strategy, that an informed analysis of the advertising text is the best way to advance our understanding of "one of the most important cultural factors moulding and reflecting our life today" (p. 11).

Of course, the issue of authorship, however broadly defined, is a familiar enough conundrum in the study of art and literature. In the context of commercial institutions, however, authorship is often implicitly treated as a nonissue, given the obvious existence of significant organizational and functional constraints. For example, within the sociology of news, Chomsky (Jhally, 1997) argued that "you could find that ninety-nine percent of the journalists are members of the Socialist Workers Party ... and that in itself would prove nothing about the media's output." For Chomsky, the form and content of news is largely dependent on issues of ownership and control.

The scholarly evidence available suggests that the critical study of advertising has been overwhelmingly biased in favor of textual approaches. This bias may simply be a matter of priorities. At the limit, however, important questions remain unspoken and unanswered. In this article, I argue not for a theory of advertising or design authorship per se; rather, I suggest that an appreciation of this commercial "culture of production" (du Gay, 1997), however inconsequential it may appear to our understanding of ideology, strengthens the explanatory force of critical cultural inquiry, understood as a holistic practice involving various points of entry, modes of analysis, and types of intervention.

Although my focus is on ad creatives and designers, my aim is not merely to democratize our research agendas, perhaps adding commercial cultural production to the existing, prevalent concentration on the text and reception. I do not even maintain that these particular cultural workers hold the key to origination or ultimate authorial intention, although I maintain that their role in the advertising and design process is of primary importance. Instead, by working against the narrow approach advocated by Williamson (1978), I hope to show the ways in which such workers embody some remarkable paradoxes, not least of which is their primary attentiveness to an audience of peers rather than a putative set of consumers at large. Furthermore, the class position and dynamic of these particular workers can be understood as characterized by uncertainty and instability, making the notion that advertising and design are a homogeneous force—a "culture industry" (Adorno & Horkheimer, 1973)—that much harder to justify or accept.

A MODEL: THE CIRCUIT OF CULTURE

In an interview, Williams (Williams, Heath, & Skirrow, 1986) made the following statement:

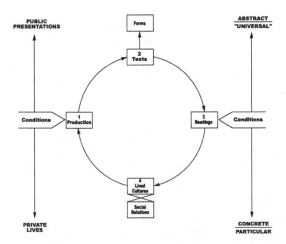

FIGURE 1   A theoretical model: The circuit of culture. Richard Johnson, "What is Cultural Studies Anyway?" *Social Text* 16 (1986/1987), p. 47. Copyright 1987. Reprinted by permission of Duke University Press. All rights reserved.

There needs to be developed many different kinds of analysis which are in touch with each other ... the least developed ... is that which tries to understand precisely the production of certain conventions and modes of communication right inside the form. I would put this at the top of the list not because it could answer all the questions on the table, but because it's the least likely thing to happen. (p.14)

That same year Johnson (1986/1987) proposed, under the title "What is Cultural Studies Anyway?" a theoretical model called the circuit of culture (see Figure 1).[1] Although not necessarily a comment on or even a response to Williams's (Williams et al., 1986) statement, the circuit offered a way to bring together the "different kinds of analysis" (p. 14) to which Williams alluded. More important, Johnson recognized that no single approach, and hence no single vantage point on his circuit, can in itself provide the kind of far-reaching analysis that, for him, constituted cultural studies. As I hope to show, the circuit also provides an excellent way of bringing to light those items on Williams's list that have, historically, been the least likely to happen.

The model indicates that we must take account of all four moments identified by Johnson: production, text, consumption, "lived cultures" and "social relations" (Johnson, 1986/1987, p. 47). I argue here that the study of advertising in particular has concentrated largely on the text and that scholarly attention to commercial cultural production has been significantly underdeveloped.[2] As Williams et al. (1986)

---

[1]The circuit has recently appeared elsewhere in slightly modified form (e.g., du Gay, Hall, Janes, Mackay, & Negus, 1997, p. 3).

[2]Although political economy has been exceedingly important in illuminating the realm of production in terms of matters such as ownership and control, it has been criticized by cultural studies scholars

suggested, attending to the "production of certain conventions and modes of com-munication" (p. 14) remains, for a variety of reasons, an underexplored, obscured, and even maligned strategy.

Hall's (1980) important article "Encoding/Decoding" may serve to highlight my basic point here: We have witnessed the emergence of audience research within cultural studies and associated concerns with the myriad issues of cultural recep-tion—in short, decoding. Hall's essay has been particularly influential in this re-spect, yet the first half of his couplet (i.e., encoding) cannot be said to have helped to foster a similarly fruitful line of inquiry, let alone a canon.

An emphasis on issues concerning the text and its reception has led to the explo-ration of our amusements, preoccupations, fears, allegiances, and pleasures—that is, on meaning-making outside the realm of work. This has often been a purposeful and, indeed, fruitful strategy in scholarly research, but it has also led, perhaps un-consciously, to a cumulative disregard for that sizeable and formative chunk of time most people devote to labor. Furthermore, this activity is not necessarily outside the scope of cultural studies.

Recent studies have begun to demonstrate the value of exploring these appar-ently unpromising arenas of research. On the advertising and design front, work on the realm of production by du Gay (1996, 1997), Nixon (1997a, 1997b), Mort (1996), and Crafton Smith (1994), among others, has led the way in opening up im-portant, heretofore neglected possibilities for fruitful cultural inquiry.[3]

In this article, I seek to strengthen the least explored sections of the circuit by drawing specific attention to the subjective aspects of commercial cultural produc-tion.[4] In the spirit of Johnson's (1986/1987) intervention, I also propose an adapta-tion of the model[5] that may provide a better account of the activities of ad personnel, particularly copywriters and art directors, and graphic designers. Ultimately, my argument is intended to apply to a whole range of workers,[6] collectively identified by Bourdieu (1984) as the "new cultural intermediaries" (p. 366).

---

for reductive or economistic tendencies. For an example that is perhaps illustrative of the contemporary and historical limitations of both political economy and cultural studies, see the colloquy in *Critical Studies in Mass Communication* (Gandy, 1995).

[3]Formal objections to such an approach are numerous. Not least is the question of whether these "elite communicators" (Marchand, 1985, p. xix) constitute a social milieu worthy of attention because they are neither subordinated nor subjugated—in fact, quite the reverse.

[4]In an extended example, Johnson (1986/1987) focused on the conception, design, production, mar-keting, and reception of a new compact car.

[5]Originally proposed in Soar (1996).

[6]A provisional list might include packaging, fashion, stage, set, industrial, and retail/window-dis-play designers; fashion and style journalists; photographers; film and TV directors; screenwriters; illus-trators; animators; model makers; typographers; actors, models, and popular musicians; and computer animators and web-page designers.

ON SEMIOTICS

Auteurism is surely dead, but so are the debates over the death of the author. In the current climate, few people would doubt the value of asking: Who is writing? or Who is speaking?

—Naremore (1990, p. 20)

Advertisements, if we take them seriously and collectively as a social and cultural phenomenon, are a rich source of ideas, both about and for the world we inhabit—albeit habitually rarefied, heavily mediated, and often distorted. Leiss, Kline, and Jhally (1990) referred to them collectively as "the privileged discourse for the circulation of messages and social cues about the interplay between persons and objects" (p. 50). Scholars of many persuasions have turned to ads to illuminate and develop their research. Ads have been classified historically (Lears, 1994; Leiss et al., 1990; Marchand, 1985); analyzed according to product category, such as cigarettes (Pollay, Lee, & Carter-Whitney, 1992), toys (Kline, 1993), jeans (Goldman, 1992), television (Spigel, 1991), cosmetics (Peiss, 1998), refrigerators (Isenstadt, 1998), or political valence (Myers, 1986); assessed for their underlying ideological or fetishistic inflexions (Ewen, 1988; Jhally, 1989); and scrutinized according to their specific portrayal of the family (Goffman, 1979), men (Katz, 1995; Wernick, 1991), women (Barthel, 1988; Clark, 1993; Goldman, 1992; Williamson, 1986), children (Seiter, 1995), and the "Other" (Kern-Foxworth, 1994; O'Barr, 1994).[7]

Williamson (1978) produced probably the best known and most referenced work on the signifying practices embedded in advertisements. Its text-centered orthodoxy (and concurrent militantism toward authorship) was informed by the work of Barthes (1977), who, as a leading semiotician, warned against any attempt to account for the supposed intentions of the producers (i.e., authors) of any message (i.e., text). Barthes asserted that "to try to find the 'sources', the 'influences' of a work, is to fall in with the myth of filiation" (p. 160). As Leiss et al. (1990) explained, "From the outset, semiologists have concentrated on relationships among the parts of a message or communication system, for, they contend, it is only through the interaction of component parts that meaning is formed" (p. 198).

The danger is that, at the limit, such work "tend[s] to derive an 'account' of readership, in fact, from the critic's own textual readings" (Johnson 1986/1987, p. 63). Perhaps the most important elision is that by following the semiotician's logic, we

---

[7]I am aware of the danger of merely being reductive here. My intention in compiling this list is simply to show that it is most often advertising texts that are organized and analyzed in the pursuit and exploration of vital cultural and social issues, rather than the realm of ad production. The selection of the former as an avenue of research cannot simply be understood as a matter of convenience, although this must surely be a latent factor. I, too, have discovered that it is remarkably difficult to gain sustained and reliable access to advertising professionals.

are then unable to account for change: Because any notion of putative authorship is ruled out of bounds, there is no credible way to explain, for example, how the strategies and content of advertising messages have developed over the last century (e.g., see the four historical stages in Leiss et al., 1990).

I am not arguing against the usefulness of semiotics—far from it. Rather, I subscribe to the notion of a theoretical and methodological agnosticism[8] that, for example, recognizes the enormous analytic power of semiotics but refuses the dogmatic overtures that have often attended it. To illustrate: Leiss et al. (1990) developed a method for ad analysis that combines semiotics with content analysis; apart from anything else, this method provides a more accessible foothold for those attempting to follow or repeat the work. However, at one extreme, the danger always remains that, as Slater (1989) suggested, "[s]uch theories are then used to ignore the actual social practice of advertising, implying instead that the ideological structure of language itself can account for the specific character of advertisements" (p. 122).

BEYOND DEAD AUTHORS: ADVERTISING
AS CULTURAL PRODUCTION

In this section, I draw on one of Hall's (1972) lesser known essays, which, properly speaking, belongs to the literature on the sociology of news. This well-established area of research provides a useful analogy for the study of commercial cultural production. Hall provided a dissection of the process of news production, with particular emphasis on the use of images. Informed by the work of Althusser and Barthes, Hall's argument stressed both the ideological underpinnings of this site of cultural production and, via semiotics, the already-inscribed nature of its output. In this compelling frame, the process of newsmaking is neither arbitrary nor purely denotative.

Hall's (1972) work can also be distinguished in other important ways. For example, Hall made room for subjective influences: the possibility that the semiformal culture of journalism may have some effect on news agendas, or at least on the way in which selected stories are framed. Hall referred, briefly, to the "social practices" or "relations" (p. 60) of news production. I adapt this part of his analysis to understand the processes of advertising and design production. To this end, it is suggested at the outset that ad agencies and especially creative departments bear comparison with the archetypal newsroom that appears in Hall's essay. The analogy it offers is therefore partial but no less informative.

The "'ritual practices' of news production" are "the actual routines by which the 'labour' of signification is ordered and regulated" (Hall, 1972, p. 61). These, in turn, are framed by a "routinized and habituated professional 'know-how'" (p. 61), by which Hall meant "certain types of knowledge ... which enable the signifying

---

[8]I am indebted to Sut Jhally for this insight.

process to take place" (p. 61). The routines of news production are analogous to the ad creatives' craft: their practical ability to produce copy (i.e., text) and layouts (i.e., sketches of how the ad may look) and to bring together the various service functions to produce an ad, including the talents of illustrators, photographers, typographers, and film crews. These activities are informed by a professional knowledge, a higher order expertise that manifests itself in the way in which the various elements are combined. This is not, of course, merely a function of each ad creative's own whims but a complex blend of constraints and influences.[9] However, this combination of practices—in sum, the "professional competence" (Hall, 1972, p. 61) of the ad creatives–overlooks one vital aspect of their work.

News production begins with events in the real world, regardless of whether these events are emphasized out of proportion to their potential significance or even ignored entirely. In his article, Hall (1972, pp. 61–64) broke down the "signifying process" into successive stages, along with the various competencies associated with each stage. Ad production, on the other hand, is not so much an accumulation of significations as an eruption, because the ad creative invents a story where none existed before. This is why the creative is possibly the most important actor, ideologically speaking, in the production of ads. Offering up concepts as if by magic, the ad creative's work is then reified through the routines of the agency around him.[10] In this sense, his output is analogous to the news event in Hall's frame, although ad creatives in particular may routinely provide a number of stories (i.e., concepts) from which one is finally chosen through various bureaucratic processes.

My argument is an attempt to raise a number of questions, such as how ideas are produced, how well the process can be explained, the influences (if any) that are at play, the investment that creatives and designers have in their own accounts of the process, and the ways in which these views may be affected by evidence of the less salutary efforts of the advertising and design communities. To begin to address these issues, it is important to assess ad creatives and designers not just as eminent individuals, be they celebrated mavericks[11] or even auteurs, but as a social stratum.

---

[9]This includes knowledge of current trends in the look of ads (and of films, magazines, etc.); an understanding, largely the result of experience, of how the ad concept will look once it has been printed in a newspaper or shot for a commercial and therefore what will work technically; an intuition about what will appeal to the audience in terms of stylization, tone of voice, pacing, use of humor, cultural references (such as the use of celebrities or inside jokes), and so on.

[10]There are still very few women working in the creative departments of ad agencies (e.g., see Kazenoff & Vagnoni, 1997), whereas women working in design have historically faired much better. The convention I have adopted is to use the masculine pronoun when referring to ad people to emphasize this vast inequity.

[11]I have in mind such luminaries as Howard Gossage (1986), Bill Bernbach (e.g., see Levenson, 1987; cf. Frank, 1997), and most recently the late Tibor Kalman (celebrated in Hall & Bierut, 1998). Although their contributions and attendant biographies often make for fascinating reading, it has yet to be established how representative they are of the rank and file professionals who remain largely unknown.

I do this first theoretically and then move on to the results of some exploratory empirical research that draws together interviews with nine individuals.

THE "CHILDREN OF MARX AND COCA-COLA": A BRIEF HISTORY OF THE CULTURAL INTERMEDIARIES

[The "flexecutives"] know how hip, British pop culture works, and because they have hung on to it long enough to see it wasn't going to cause a revolution, they can sell the knowledge with a clear conscience. They're largely why the mainstream appropriates the underground so quickly now—there's a fifth column of thirtysomethings selling the battle plans to the businessmen and politicians—who are eager to buy, of course, because hip youth culture is "new" and "old" doesn't work.

—Benson (1999, p. 2)

It is now 25 years since Bell (1976) set out to explain the "cultural contradictions of capitalism." His concern was, according to Lee (1993), with the danger posed by a "generally hedonistic, spendthrift and throw-away ethic" (p. 106). Capitalism, as a long-established economic system, had "always been fuelled by certain ascetic principles of self-denial" (p.106), which ensured that there was constant and sufficient reinvestment in mass production. However, in light of the characteristically excessive tendencies of mass consumption, the perpetuation of investment might ultimately be insufficient to ensure capital's stability.

In his thesis, Bell (1976) identified a social constituency he referred to as the "cultural mass," whose members were mainly to be found "in the knowledge and communications industries [and] who, with their families, would number several million persons" (p. 20n). Inner circles within this group were to be distinguished further by their particularly heightened cultural attunement. Bell's inventory included "writers ... movie-makers, musicians" and those in "higher education, publishing, magazines, broadcast media, theater, and museums" (p. 20n). He located the emergence of this loose affiliation in the decline of the avant garde:

Today modernism is exhausted. There is no tension. The creative impulses have gone slack. It has become an empty vessel. The impulse to rebellion has been institutionalized by the "cultural mass" and its experimental forms have become the syntax and semiotics of advertising and haute couture. (p. 20)

This appropriately named mass (unfairly) enjoys the status of artists and the trappings of bourgeois society: They have "the luxury of 'freer' lifestyles while holding comfortable jobs" (Bell, 1976, p. 20). Moreover, they are "not the creators of culture but the *transmitters*" (Bell, 1976, p. 20n); they merely "process and influence the reception of serious cultural products" (Bell, 1976, p. 20n), and only then does this group "produce the popular materials for the wider mass-culture audience" (Bell, 1976, p. 20n).

The relative legitimacy of the cultural mass appears to depend on how the particular formulation of this shift is conceived. For example, a more positive conceptualization is to be found in the work of Featherstone (1991). Reworking and updating Bell's (1976) assertions, he characterized the new cultural intermediaries[12] as "those in media, design, fashion, advertising, and 'para' intellectual information occupations, whose jobs entail performing services and the production, marketing and dissemination of symbolic goods" (p. 19). It is important to note, however, that whereas for Bell the so-called cultural mass seems to emerge as an effect of the "corrosive force" (Featherstone, 1991, p. 8) of modernism, for Featherstone, the new cultural intermediaries are rather more significant, if not instrumentally involved. Indeed, for McGuigan (1992), at least, "Featherstone argues convincingly that postmodernism is primarily to be understood ... as the product of the 'new cultural intermediaries' and perhaps only secondarily, or at second hand, as a truly popular phenomenon" (p. 216).

McGuigan (1992), for his part, asserted that the intermediaries have emerged from the "radical middle-class youth of the 1960s" (p. 218), although for them "'[r]esistance' is reduced to the knowing consumption of consumer products" (Callinicos, 1989, p.170). Their fate was summed up in the caustic comment—after Godard[13]—that they are best seen as the "children of Marx and Coca Cola" (Callinicos, 1989, p. 170; see also Lee, 1993, p. 107). Featherstone (1991), too, maintained that the class of intermediaries "includes those from the counterculture who have survived from the 1960s and those who have taken up elements of their cultural imagery in different contexts" (p. 21).

FROM COMMERCIAL ARTISTS TO CULTURAL INTERMEDIARIES

We are now in a position to consider advertisements, logos, brochures, commercials, compact disc covers, and so forth as the contrived and somewhat reflective

---

[12]This is my preferred term, given the dubious overtones of Bell's (1976) nebulous cultural mass. It is also the most commonly used and inclusive moniker amongst many alternatives (with varying degrees of relevance), some of which are: new petite bourgeoisie (Bourdieu, 1984); the service class, the new (postmodern) class fraction (Lash & Urry, 1987); cultural specialists, cultural entrepreneurs, para-intellectuals, symbolic specialists, new tastemakers (Featherstone, 1991); flexecutives (Benson, 1999). See also Lee (1993).

[13]Godard (1966) coined this phrase in reference to the young French characters in his film *Masculin-Féminin*.

communications of an obscure elite, whose members continually attempt to bridge the paradox between their artistic impulses and the economic constraints to which they are tied. Harvey (1991) characterized creatives by the slightly sinister trait of feeding on "serious cultural products" and then producing (excreting?) "popular materials for the wider mass-culture audience" (p. 68). Featherstone (1991), although acknowledging that they may indeed "ransack various traditions and cultures" (p. 19), detected a certain predicament in propagating their "elite provincialism" (Marchand, 1985, p. xvii):

> Their habitus, dispositions and lifestyle preferences are such that they identify with artists and intellectuals, yet under conditions of the demonopolization of artistic and intellectual commodity enclaves they have the apparent contradictory interests of sustaining the prestige and cultural capital of these enclaves, while at the same time popularizing and making them more accessible to wider audiences. (Featherstone, 1991, p. 19)

We may thus contrast a conception of ad creatives (and designers, etc.) as culture vultures (via Harvey, 1991) with the notion of cultured vultures (via Featherstone, 1991). Both formulations compare favorably with Lears's (1994) description of the "extraordinarily talented people" (p. 262) who have been associated with advertising:

> These artists and writers have served, in a sense, as emissaries between social universes: the agency–client world and the wider population; art and big business; museum and commercial culture. They have worked various boundaries, sometimes creatively reconnecting aesthetics and everyday life, more often conforming out of necessity to the constraints of agency organization. (p. 262)

The members of this class fraction "are forced to invent the skillfully ambiguous discourses and practices that were, so to speak, inscribed in advance in the very definition of [their] position" (Bourdieu, 1984, p. 366n) as both constituents of a fraction characterized by the work it performs, involving "presentation and representation" (p. 359), and as consumers, that is, class fraction and taste culture:

> the new petite bourgeoisie is predisposed to play a vanguard role in the struggles over everything concerned with the art of living, in particular, domestic life and consumption, relations between the sexes and the generations, the reproduction of the family and its values. (Bourdieu, 1984, p. 366; also quoted in Bonner & du Gay, 1992, p. 177)

This vanguard role is achieved and maintained most forcefully through the values and attitudes purveyed through advertising and design images and through which the intermediaries can most clearly be understood as having an authorial function.

PROFESSIONAL PERSPECTIVES ON ADVERTISING
AND DESIGN PRODUCTION

To understand better the influences, expectations, and aspirations of the intermediaries and how these supplement the theoretical accounts so far developed, in this section, I turn to a consideration of the creative workers to be found in the businesses of design and advertising. Although they rarely wear their ideological contradictions on their sleeves (as do their fictional counterparts[14]), ad creatives and designers nevertheless embody a very particular paradox. Although habitually laying claim to the spontaneity, freedom of expression, and originality that the term *creative* implies, they are also ideological participants whose professional routines demarcate their output in very precise terms.

These intermediaries are constituted as an ever-vigilant audience through their professional appetite for media products. Indeed, as I have argued, there is some connection between the cultural and social experiences of copywriters, art directors, and graphic designers and the apparently spontaneous solutions they provide on a daily basis for the clients their organizations serve, quite apart from some putative audience.[15]

Methodology

The empirical research presented here is drawn from a total of nine interviews. Five were conducted in 1993[16] in Los Angeles, and the others were conducted in New York and Massachusetts in 1997. These interviews are contextualized with secondary sources such as excerpts from other interviews (Hirschman, 1989; Schudson, 1993; Shapiro, 1981; see also, Frank, 1997; Hirota, 1995; Lewis, 1964; Slater, 1985; Tunstall, 1964) and trade articles. I also draw, implicitly at least, on my own experience as a graphic designer and art director.[17] The earlier interviews were with senior ad creatives (Bert, John, Steve, Colin, and Rick[18]), who provided some authoritative views on the professional beliefs and day-to-day activities of established art directors and copywriters. The more recent set of interviews deals with two ad creatives (Mike and Ben) and two graphic designers (Mary and Karl) and was part of an ongoing effort to extend my research beyond advertising to another major

---

[14]See, for example the films *How to Get Ahead in Advertising* (Robinson, 1989) and *Bliss* (Lawrence, 1985).

[15]As Marchand (1985) noted, "Not only were [ad creators] likely to portray the world they knew, rather than the world experienced by typical citizens ... they sometimes allowed their cultural preferences to influence their depiction of society" (p. xvii).

[16]I am indebted to Sut Jhally and Steve Kline for the use of this material.

[17]I trained and then worked as an art director and graphic designer in London from 1989 to 1993 and have continued to do so in the United States since 1996.

[18]All names used are pseudonyms.

professional group of cultural intermediaries. In this article, I focus mainly on their comments about working methods and attitudes toward potential criticisms of their output.

Eight of the nine interviewees are White men, most middle aged (although the youngest is 29), all with extensive educations: John has a degree in journalism with a minor in advertising, Steve has a double major in English and marketing, Colin took a marketing degree with a minor in advertising, and Rick has a graduate degree in English. Mary and Karl are successful graphic designers who run their own businesses: Mary is self-employed, complementing her design work with advertising, depending on client needs; Karl is a creative director and has a large staff working mainly on a folio of mass-circulation, family-oriented magazines. Based on their levels of experience, all interviewees can be described, in industry parlance, as middleweights or heavyweights. Indeed, the five men interviewed in 1993 had all attained at least the senior rank of creative director. The participants were all very forthcoming, often using anecdotes, examples, and jokes to illustrate their comments.

My findings rarely contradict the empirical evidence presented in other studies (e.g., Hirota, 1995; Hirschman, 1989; Schudson, 1993; Shapiro, 1981; Slater, 1985, 1989) although the arguments they support may differ significantly. Moreover, the degree of fit with the beliefs expressed by ad creatives and even the way in which these are phrased in other studies has, at times, been almost uncanny. For the sake of brevity, therefore, the evidence presented here is limited to that which directly impinges on the thesis at hand.

The Role of Organic Research

The preferred criteria by which creatives assess the worth of advertisements and commercials (both their own and others') are expressly not those imposed from outside: Any kind of quantitative research that seeks to establish an objective evaluation on completed work—known as testing the creative—is vehemently renounced by the participants; according to Steve, "no truly innovative idea can ever be tested if it's truly innovative because people won't know how to react to it."[19]

According to Rick, the information provided in creative briefs, including psychographic and demographic profiles, appears to be used only as a touchstone once the process of invention is underway (see also Shapiro, 1981, p. 370). Creatives may also seek out personal views, canvassing public opinion (in this example, about the particular product category in which the interviewee works): "I like to talk to people at the gas pump. You know: 'Nice truck. Why did you buy it?'"

---

[19]This sentiment is not uncommon and is faithfully echoed by ad man Robert Pritikin, in interview with Schudson (1993, p. 83).

(Rick). Ben mentioned having recently looked at an article in *Time* magazine; Mary remembered being "inspired by" a wall display in a university hallway.

Aside from the more obvious examples of practical research such as this, there is a further and greatly significant source. Rick's comment about the truck continued thus: "It's fun: we're all consumers, we're all consuming something at any point in life." Here is evidence for the assertion that creatives draw on their experience as consumers at least as much as any acumen they accumulate through their lives on the job. Formal training is neither a necessity nor a norm. As one of Schudson's (1993) participants commented, "I don't know anything now, after twelve years in the business, I didn't know when I began, except some technique" (p. 85).

Shapiro's (1981) ethnographic study of four advertising agencies includes many references to the functional importance of the "aesthetic tastes and idiosyncratic assumptions held by the creatives" (p. 278). This reliance on "anything they encounter—in their personal lives as well as in the work setting" (p. 277) runs from the obvious, such as casting sessions (e.g., a particular woman was chosen to appear in a commercial because "the men responsible ... found her attractive and ... thought that most people in the audience would also" [p. 83]), to using the product (e.g., "to find benefits that they can then tell consumers about, based on their own experiences" [p. 48]). In the words of Mike, ad creatives "need to understand their time; what the things are that are motivating people today, what people respond to today, what people worry about today, what people think is important today." Ben commented that "advertising picks up on the movies"; for Colin, "if I see something interesting, if I see some technique done in a movie, I will always apply that to an advertisement ... [from] the regular Hollywood, all the way down to the obscure foreign films which are not so popular but you can preen elements from that."[20] Gordon Thompson III, Vice President of research, design, and development at Nike said: "The best designers always know what's going on in the world. We know what's going on in film, in sports, in fashion—where all of the trends are going" (as cited in Vanderbilt, 1998, p. 58). According to John, another ad man, "it's inventing a new technique: inventing something in your head and then getting someone to go and do it. It's these new fictions." The fictions are ads that, rather than being derivative, he saw as entirely original: "When someone does it, and when it does work, it puts you so far above everyone else, so out-distances everyone else, that the power is just unbelievable."

This organic research begins with ads on TV, on the radio, and in magazines, but, at its most intense, there is an expressed need for total immersion in the cultural environment: "Within my creative department you can't name a movie, foreign or

---

[20]This is perfectly illustrated by the emergence of morphing, an advanced computer technique that gives the appearance of one object metamorphosing into another, on-screen. This technique had been popularized in the movie *Terminator 2* (Cameron, 1991) and was mentioned by nearly all the interviewees as a fad because it had already become overused in advertising.

domestic, that someone here hasn't seen; a book that someone hasn't read. People in our industry thrive on stimulus. We're pretty much in touch" (John); "You have to be a cultural junkie. It's not just media, but it's radio, it's art, fashion, walking down the street, not living in one place, traveling" (Steve).

Assessing Quality: The Importance of Creativity

The creative directors interviewed are clearly concerned with safeguarding the quality of output of their departments, and this is measured in a very particular way, as Colin argued:

> if you talk to most creatives, they're always striving to be original. They're striving to create something that is unlike anything else that is on the air. It becomes part of your everyday existence, and so it becomes a given; a mandate; or a credo, and there are some agencies where creativity has nothing to do with it. It really depends on who you talk to. I would say that most good creatives are always striving to be different.

Creativity, therefore, appears to be practically and ideologically a very powerful notion. According to my interviewees, who generally agreed on most matters, the creative contribution is indeed pivotal. As Ben asserted: "The creative is the product, and there's nothing in this business without it." Furthermore, there is little doubt in anyone's mind that a creative ad is a successful ad. The reverse is also true: In response to a question about good ads and bad ads, they all associated the good one with creative achievement and the bad one with external interference or incompetence. When asked, "What do you think when you see a good ad?" a typical response (given here by Ben) was "Jeez, that was a good idea"; Mary added, "I just am awed by the fact that people continually come up with brilliant, creative ideas." However, when asked, "What do you think when you see a bad ad?" the frame of reference changed noticeably. Ben stated, "Boy, how'd they ever sell that to a client?" and "How could anyone ever have bought this?" Mary's response was, "Oh, wow, people are spending money on that—I can't believe it."

It appears that, for these creatives, a good ad is in fact a well-conceived idea for which the creative person can take direct credit. For Mary a good ad is evidence of "a client that allowed a creative to do their job," as opposed to money well spent or an ad expertly placed in the media or professionally managed. Furthermore, a bad ad is evidence, a priori, of a bad client, lousy account handling, or wasted money. Nowhere was it suggested that a bad ad may be the result of poor creative work (i.e., bad creative or a bad idea).

There is also a major emphasis on creativity as a transcendent, ethereal process. As Karl said, "I just know that the little muse is gonna show her face, before the deadline." Even Mike, my jaundiced interviewee—a 55-year-old who had relinquished day-to-day creative work for a role as a creative manager—said, "There's always something nebulous about really what they do, I suspect they don't understand it themselves particularly." Ben maintained that "there is no one-plus-one-equals-two," and Mary went to great pains to explain a process reminiscent of that of a medium at a seance: "I believe it's a matter of being open to receiving inspiration"; "I've learned to trust that it'll come ... it's just being open to it."[21]

All the responses underline the need for creatives and creativity, whether explicitly or by insinuation. More important, this valorization does not extend to the ultimate audience, the consumer. Rarely, if ever, is the discourse on good and bad ads located in the realm of effectiveness. This may be surprising were it not for the fact that award-winning work is the single most important asset that a career-minded creative can have: An award is "a measuring stick, a salary-getter" (Steve); "you make your bones, you get your award, you get some press, and then you merchandise it to get a better job" (Bert).

The evident commitment to some kind of holy grail of originality, institutionalized in a number of national and international creative awards programs, was summed up by Bert, who is the highest ranking creative director at a major international agency:

> The bottom line affects us, but there is one thing that creative people have, that the rest of the business people and the business don't have, and that's "ego gratification." To win an award in our business doesn't mean much to a client; they don't give a shit if you win an award. If anything, they'll think that's all you want to do: win awards. What they don't realize is that's the great motivation for a creative person. We're here to make a salary, but it's also to be respected by his peers for work that has made the people [i.e., consumers] hopeful, made the people crazy.

This view was taken to its logical extreme by two of the interviewees, who clearly feel that sales are secondary if not irrelevant. When asked if effectiveness is a criteria for brilliance, John replied,

> No. I think that creative people admire a lot of advertising and they don't really care if it's successful in a pure sense of whether it moved products off the shelves. I think creative people look at advertising in a pure sense. Do they think it's a fresh approach.

In consideration of a question regarding the criteria used to judge the submissions for creative awards competitions, Steve said, "What they call great advertising, I would call great advertising. It has nothing to do with sales. It has to do with what's the work like, how does it feel?" The experienced art director interviewed by

---

[21]This introverted approach is apparently favored by very few creative types, and Steve refered to it derisively as the Trappist monk theory: "See nothing and do nothing and have it all come from within." He added, "personally I'll think that the most subscribe to *my* school. I hire that way."

Hirschman (1989) responded to potential criticism of such motives thus: "My attitude is that whatever is good for [me] is good for the client!" (p. 47).

The apparent chasm between the pursuit of sales effectiveness and creative excellence is particularly noticeable in the orientation of awards schemes. Whereas creatives clearly value ads themselves, clients generally do not; in sum, effectiveness and creative innovation can be achieved independently of one another, "due to the *varied personal utilities* of the produced advertisement" (Hirschman, 1989, pp. 42–43; italics added). At least one interviewee reiterated the generally regarded belief that these two categories tend to produce mutually exclusive winners, although "occasionally the same advertisement may fulfill both sets of goals"[22] (p. 51). The picture that begins to emerge is of a microculture within the advertising industry that clearly functions at a tangent to the supposed mission of the business as a whole.

AD GENESIS: THE SHORT CIRCUIT

The primary audience of consumers was so distant, and evidences of its approval so impersonal and uncertain, that the creative elite became heavily dependent on this secondary audience of colleagues ... the most powerful audience was other advertising professionals.

—Marchand (1985, p. 82)

The argument has been made that there is a pedagogic function in advertising and design, in which private codes are disseminated to a broader cultural mass via the creatives. As perfect consumers operating in a particularly rarefied social milieu, their own cultural readings are highly attuned. They also consume ads and design concepts written by other people, sometimes in hypercritical ways; they consume award-winning and controversial campaigns; and they gravitate toward any number of fashionable cultural watering holes that provide sustenance, inspiration, or even rip-off material. These sources are inevitably subject to a high level of turnover in the constant movement toward new experiences, styles, or graphic looks but have included magazines such as *The Face*, club culture, and film or music scenes.

Given this assertion, Johnson's (1986/1987) description of lived cultures—formerly assumed to refer to consumers in general—takes on a very particular significance. He wrote of:

---

[22]This is an eternally contentious point, and one that a recent international survey by Donald Gunn of the Leo Burnett Agency attempted to settle. His conclusion was that "an award-winning ad is more than two-and-a-half times more likely to sell than one that is not, using an established Burnett maxim that only a third of brands have a growing market share at any one time" (Martin, 1995, pp. 34–35).

the existing ensembles of cultural elements already active within particular social milieux … and the social relations on which these combinations depend. These reservoirs of discourses and meanings are in turn raw material for fresh cultural production. They are indeed among the specifically cultural conditions of production. (p. 47)

The so-called children of Marx and Coca-Cola can finally be located as a producing and consuming cohort that acts, at least in the latter realm, as an autonomous, or self-addressing entity. The members of this group draw sustenance from their own ranks, that is, from the work of other cultural intermediaries. Collaboration among them is common. Art directors habitually call on the expertise of photographers, illustrators, and typographers; photographers work with stylists, models, and model makers; producers of films, ads, and TV shows depend on orchestrated collaborations of writers, art directors, actors, set designers, costume designers, model makers, musicians, and animators. A second level of activity involves the handling, sometimes at a distance, of one intermediary's work by several others. Advertising is again an illuminating example: The creative team provides a promotional platform for a commodity that probably has already been the result of successive involvements by product or industrial designers and their model makers and then by packaging designers with illustrators, photographers, and typographers. The work of the ad creatives may then be augmented by other promotional activities such as in-store displays involving point-of-sale designers and retail and shop-window designers, sales promotions involving art directors and copywriters working with a similar number of intermediaries, direct marketing involving art directors, copywriters, and even web-page designers.

In Johnson's (1986/1987) formulation, the circuit (see Figure 1) represented a way of understanding "the production and circulation of subjective forms" (p. 47). It also concerned, in its latter moment, the realm of public consumption, and by inference an unspecified consumer. I have understood "reading or cultural consumption as a production process in which the first product becomes a material for fresh labour"; that is, from "text-as-produced" to "text-as-read" (p. 58). However, my claim is that we can also consider a secondary, privatized loop that falls short of the more usual pattern. This I call the short circuit (see Figure 2), and it is one in which the cultural intermediaries act as producers and consumers. This circuit of meaning is short in two senses: Most obviously it is faster, suggesting that the cultural capital so carried is channeled back around to the intermediaries en masse long before it works its way into and through the public domain; furthermore, the notion of an electrical short circuit provides for the idea that this attenuated arrangement is perhaps detrimental to the functionality of Johnson's larger, more conventional circuit.

I readily acknowledge that, in countering the conflation of text and production, there is an attendant danger of conflating creativity with originality. This is, to my mind, a pitfall we would do well to avoid. As it happens, Barthes (1981) reminded us that

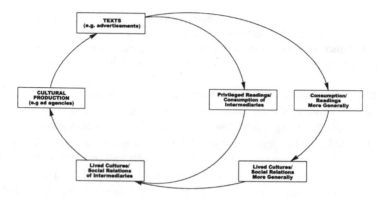

FIGURE 2   The short circuit. Based on Johnson's (1986/1987) *Circuit of Culture.*

a text is ... a variety of writings, none of them original. ... a tissue of quotations drawn from the innumerable centres of culture. ... the writer can only imitate a gesture that is always anterior, never original. ... the inner "thing" he thinks to "translate" is itself only a ready-formed dictionary, its words only explainable through other words, and so on indefinitely ... (p. 211)

Having at the outset rejected the dogmatic overtures of semiotics, I think we can still draw a valuable lesson from Barthes's (1981) assertion. Although it is conceivable that an ad creative or designer may see his or her own work as entirely without precedent, the fact remains that there are fundamental expectations among clients, ad executives, and audiences that make such an absolutist position untenable, if not plain ludicrous. My view is that we can treat these putative authors as neither dead nor omnipotent. Similarly, their output is no more derivative of a ready-formed dictionary than it is conjured up from the ether, *sui generis.*

A clue to the resultant conundrum may lie in the habitual claims made in the name of creativity. At the limit, I argue that this capacity or gift, this frustratingly nebulous process, simply acts as a kind of ideological smokescreen: It shields the intermediaries, particularly ad creatives, from the potential epiphany that their endeavors may merely be the prosaic, artless instruments of capital accumulation, and it deflects societal scrutiny away from the self-same discovery, planting it instead in the ever-attractive spectacle of charisma, showmanship, and entertainment.

Furthermore, the distinct impression given in the interviews is that these people are all, paradoxically, unique and original thinkers, a community of mavericks. This may be necessary because the alternative is for them to understand themselves as part of a process, a systematic set of representations in which individual ads are not so much personal gestures as ideologically predetermined contributions to the "discourse through and about objects" (Leiss et al., 1990, p. 5). It is perhaps this paradox, above all, that deserves further investigation.

CONCLUSIONS

The study of visual form and language is limited if it does not consider the forces of cultural production, which involve a set of social relations between producer and audience.

—Howard (1997, p. 199)

In this article I have explored the class fraction that Bourdieu (1984) identified as the cultural intermediaries. Using both theoretical and empirical lines of inquiry, I have tried to show how the intermediaries draw on their own authored array of cultural products to demarcate their cultural and social attitudes. To schematize this activity, I proposed a modified version of Johnson's (1986/1987) circuit of culture. The short circuit posits that, in terms of cultural production, the intermediaries' first audience, and hence their first source for inspiration, is themselves and their work. This effectively circumvents both consumers at large and the marketing routines to which the intermediaries ostensibly adhere to reach them. Understood as a cultural constituency, therefore, institutional constraints are of rather less consequence for our study of ad creatives; people working in ad agencies generally believe that copywriters and art directors are indeed the originators of advertisements and commercials (Hirschman, 1989), and numerous annual awards programs[23] reinforce this commonsense attitude. I have tried to show, therefore, that some critical leverage may be had from exploring a broadly conceived notion of authorship in commercial cultural production, although precisely how much leverage remains to be seen. Ultimately, the contradictions that exist between notions of structure on the one hand and agency on the other hand deserve to be investigated; we need not rely on a principled adherence to one at the expense of the other.

Members of the intermediaries occasionally publish interventions that serve to crystallize issues extending beyond the immediate realm of professional accountability and that attempt to grapple with more profound subject matter such as long-term social responsibility. One such example is the First Things First manifesto, originally drafted in 1964 by a British designer who was, along with 21 supporters, intent on countering the excesses of advertising. The manifesto was recently redrafted, with the nominal support of 33 well-known intermediaries, and published in at least six visual arts periodicals, including *Abdusters, Eye, Emigre,* and the journal of the American Institute of Graphic Arts (see Soar, 1999).

In a critical article about the original First Things First manifesto, which also helped to precipitate its renewal, Howard (1997) advocated a similarly spirited approach to working that, through "partnerships and collaborations, ... will acknowledge the link between our choices as designers and the sort of culture we wish to

---

[23]Among those currently in operation are the Art Directors Club Annual, One Show, the D&AD Awards, the *Campaign* Press Awards, the Eurobest Awards, and the Cannes Lions.

contribute to" (p. 200). Howard's is an informed intervention: He berated the evisceration of Barthes's work—"literary raiding" (p. 199)—by some schools of design and took a principled stand against Benetton, ridiculing its creative director, Oliviero Toscani, for his "unbelievably inane work" (p. 198). This is not the blithe commentary of a cultural worker oblivious to critical thinking or hopelessly mired in some unified industry position; furthermore, Howard is clearly not the only example.[24] Still, such arguments are the exception to business as usual rather than the rule; they are also more common among designers than they are among ad creatives, at least publicly so[25].

These cultural producers must be understood collectively as neither a monolithic entity nor an entirely apolitical one. From time to time some attempt the difficult task of reaching beyond an infatuation with technique and content—perhaps the least that scholars of the media and culture can do as expert witnesses with potential access to production as well as lived cultures, consumption, and the text.

Part of our task may be to extend the metaphor of advertising as a (distorted) mirror of society reflecting back on its audience because the intermediaries occupy front-row seats on both sides—production and consumption, encoding and decoding. Regardless of which side of the mirror they may lurk at any moment, the intermediaries always find themselves there first, at once flattered by the spectacle of their own work and often willfully oblivious to the audiences identified for them by the contemporary routines of marketing research.

ACKNOWLEDGMENTS

I thank Steve Kline for an earlier opportunity to explore these issues; the organizers of various conference panels for allowing me to present some of these ideas (Association for Economic & Social Analysis and Paul du Gay, in particular); Sut Jhally; my anonymous reviewers; and, finally, Matt McAllister and Sharon Mazzarella for their skilled editing suggestions.

REFERENCES

Adorno, T., & Horkheimer, M. (1973). *Dialectics of enlightenment.* London: Lane.
Barthel, D. (1988). *Putting on appearances: Gender and advertising.* Philadelphia: Temple University.
Barthes, R. (1977). *Image music text.* New York: Hill & Wang.
Barthes, R. (1981). The death of the author. In J. Caughie (Ed.), *Theories of authorship: A reader* (pp. 208–213). London: Routledge & Kegan Paul/BFI.
Bell, D. (1976). *The cultural contradictions of capitalism.* New York: Basic.

---

[24]My current research is an exploration of the multivalent characteristics of design and advertising practice, both in terms of personal values and professional politics.

[25]This is one potential avenue of research. The formal split between designers and ad creatives has been debated for many years (for a recent example, see Poynor, 1998a, 1998b).

Benson, R. (1999, February 4). Flexible friends. *The Guardian,* p. 2.

Bonner, F., & du Gay, P. (1992). *Thirtysomething* and contemporary consumer culture: Distinctiveness and distinction. In R. Burrows & C. Marsh (Eds.), *Consumption and class: Divisions and change* (pp. 166–183). London: Macmillan.

Bourdieu, P. (1984). *Distinction: A social critique of the judgement of taste* (R. Nice, Trans.). London: Routledge & Kegan Paul.

Callinicos, A. (1989). *Against postmodernism: A Marxist critique.* Cambridge, England: Polity.

Cameron, J. (Director). (1991). *Terminator 2: Judgment day* [Film]. Los Angeles: TriStar Pictures.

Clark, D. (1993). Commodity lesbianism. In H. Abelove, M. A. Barale, & D. M. Halperin (Eds.), *The lesbian and gay studies reader* (pp. 186–201). New York: Routledge.

Crafton Smith, M. (1994). Culture is the limit: Pushing the boundaries of graphic design criticism and practice. *Visible Language, 28,* 298–316.

du Gay, P. (1996). *Consumption and identity at work.* London: Sage.

du Gay, P. (Ed.). (1997). *Production of culture/cultures of production.* London: Sage/Open University.

du Gay, P., Hall, S., Janes, L., Mackay, H., & Negus, K. (1997). *Doing cultural studies: The story of the Sony walkman.* London: Sage/Open University.

Ewen, S. (1988). *All consuming images: The politics of style in contemporary culture.* New York: Basic.

Featherstone, M. (1991). *Consumer culture and postmodernism.* London: Sage.

Frank, T. (1997). *The conquest of cool: Business culture, counterculture, and the rise of hip consumerism.* Chicago: University of Chicago Press.

Gandy, O. H., Jr. (Ed.). (1995). Colloquy (Special issue). *Critical Studies in Mass Communication 12*(1).

Godard, J.-L. (Director). (1966). *Masculin, Féminin* [Film]. Anouchka Films.

Goffman, E. (1979). *Gender advertisements.* Cambridge, MA: Harvard University Press.

Goldman, R. (1992). *Reading ads socially.* London: Routledge.

Gossage, H. (1986). *Is there any hope for advertising?* Urbana: University of Illinois Press.

Hall, P., & Bierut, M. (1998). *Tibor Kalman: Perverse optimist.* Princeton, NJ: Princeton Architectural Press.

Hall, S. (1972, Autumn). The determinations of newsphotographs. *Working Papers in Cultural Studies,* 53–87.

Hall, S. (1980). "Encoding/decoding." In S. Hall, S. Baron, M. Denning, D. Hobson, A. Lowe, & P. Willis (Eds.), *Culture, media, language* (pp. 128–138). London: Hutchinson.

Harvey, D. (1991). Flexibility: Threat or opportunity? *Socialist Review, 21*(1), 65–77.

Hirota, J. (1995). Making products heroes: Work in advertising agencies. In R. Jackall (Ed.), *Propaganda* (pp. 329–350). New York: NYU Press.

Hirschman, E. C. (1989). Role-based models of advertising creation and production. *Journal of Advertising, 18*(4), 42–53.

Howard, A. (1997). There is such a thing as society. In M. Bierut, W. Drenttel, S. Heller, & D. K. Holland (Eds.), *Looking closer 2: Critical writings on graphic design* (pp. 195–200). New York: Allworth.

Isenstadt, S. (1998). Visions of plenty: Refrigerators in America around 1950. *Journal of Design History, 11,* 311–321.

Jhally, S. (1989). *The codes of advertising: Fetishism and the political economy of meaning in the consumer society.* New York: St. Martin's.

Jhally, S. (1995). Image-based culture: Advertising and popular culture. In G. Dines & J. Humez (Eds.), *Gender, race and class in media* (pp. 77–87). London: Sage.

Jhally, S. (Producer and Director). (1997). *The myth of the liberal media: The propaganda model of news* [Videotape]. (Available from the Media Education Foundation, 26 Center Street, Northampton, MA 01060)

Johnson, R. (1986/1987). What is cultural studies anyway? *Social Text, 16,* 38–80.

Katz, J. (1995). Advertising and the construction of violent white masculinity. In G. Dines & J. Humez (Eds.), *Gender, race and class in media* (pp. 133–141). London: Sage.

Kazenoff, I., & Vagnoni, A. (1997, October). Babes in boyland. *Creativity, 5*(8), 18–20.

Kern-Foxworth, M. (1994). *Aunt Jemima, Uncle Ben, & Rastus: Blacks in advertising, yesterday, today, and tomorrow.* Westport, CT: Greenwood.

Kline, S. (1993). *Out of the garden: Toys, TV, and children's culture in the age of marketing.* London: Verso.

Lash, S., & Urry, J. (1987). *The end of organized capitalism.* Cambridge, England: Polity.

Lawrence, R. (Director). (1985). *Bliss* [Film]. New South Wales Film Corp.

Lears, J. (1994). *Fables of abundance: A cultural history of advertising in America.* New York: Basic.

Lee, M. (1993). *Consumer culture reborn: The cultural politics of consumption.* London: Routledge.

Leiss, W., Kline, S., & Jhally, S. (1990). *Social communication in advertising: Persons, products and images of well-being* (2nd ed.). Scarborough: Nelson Canada.

Levenson, B. (1987). *Bill Bernbach's book: A history of the advertising that changed the history of advertising.* New York: Villard.

Lewis, I. (1964). In the courts of power: The advertising man. In P. L. Berger (Ed.), *The human shape of work: Studies in the sociology of occupations* (pp. 113–180). New York: Macmillan.

Marchand, R. (1985). *Advertising the American dream: Making way for modernity, 1920–1940.* Berkeley: University of California Press.

Martin, M. (1995, September 22). Do creative commercials sell? *Campaign,* 34–35.

McGuigan, J. (1992). *Cultural populism.* London: Routledge.

Mort, F. (1996). *Cultures of consumption: Masculinities and social space in late twentieth-century Britain.* London: Routledge.

Myers, K. (1986). *Understains: The sense and seduction of advertising.* London: Comedia.

Naremore, J. (1990). Authorship and the cultural politics of film criticism. *Film Quarterly, 44*(1), 14–22.

Nixon, S. (1997a). Advertising executives as modern men: Masculinity and the UK advertising industry in the 1980s. In M. Nava, A. Blake, I. MacRury, & B. Richards (Eds.), *Buy this book: Studies in advertising and consumption* (pp. 103–119). London: Routledge.

Nixon, S. (1997b). Circulating culture. In P. du Gay (Ed.), *Production of culture/cultures of production* (pp. 179–219). London: Sage/Open University.

O'Barr, W. (1994). *Culture and the ad: Exploring otherness in the world of advertising.* Boulder, CO: Westview.

Peiss, K. (1998). *Hope in a jar: The making of America's beauty culture.* New York: Metropolitan.

Pollay, R., Lee, J. S., & Carter-Whitney, D. (1992). Separate, but not equal: Racial segmentation in cigarette advertising. *Journal of Advertising, 21,* 45–57.

Poynor, R. (1998a). Design is advertising (Part 1). *Eye, 29,* 46–51.

Poynor, R. (1998b). Design is advertising (Part 2). *Eye, 30,* 36–43.

Robinson, B. (Director). (1989). *How to get ahead in advertising* [Film]. Handmade Films.

Schudson, M. (1993). *Advertising, the uneasy persuasion* (2nd ed.). London: Routledge.

Seiter, E. (1995). Different children, different dreams: Racial representation in advertising. In G. Dines & J. Humez (Eds.), *Gender, race and class in media* (pp. 99–108). London: Sage.

Shapiro, K. (1981). *The construction of television commercials: Four cases of interorganizational problem-solving.* Unpublished doctoral dissertation, Stanford University.

Slater, D. (1985). *Advertising as a commercial practice: Business strategy and social theory.* Unpublished doctoral dissertation, Cambridge University, London.

Slater, D. (1989). Corridors of power. In J. F. Gubrium & D. Silverman (Eds.), *The politics of field research: Sociology beyond enlightenment* (pp. 113–131). London: Sage.

Soar, M. (1996). *"The children of Marx and Coca-Cola": Advertising and commercial creativity.* Unpublished masters thesis, Simon Fraser University, Burnaby, Canada.

Soar, M. (1999). The impotence of being earnest. *AIGA Journal of Graphic Design, 17*(3), 6–7.

Spigel, L. (1991). The domestic economy of television viewing in postwar America. In R. Avery & D. Eason (Eds.), *Critical perspectives on media and society* (pp. 387–405). New York: Guilford.

Tunstall, J. (1964). *The advertising man in London advertising agencies.* London: Chapman & Hall.

Vanderbilt, T. (1998). *The sneaker book: Anatomy of an industry and an icon.* New York: New Press.

Wernick, A. (1991). *Promotional culture: Advertising, ideology and symbolic expression.* London: Sage.

Williams, R., Heath, S., & Skirrow, G. (1986). An interview with Raymond Williams. In T. Modleski (Ed.), *Studies in entertainment: Critical approaches to mass culture* (pp. 3–17). Bloomington: Indiana University Press.

Williamson, J. (1978). *Decoding advertisements: Ideology and meaning in advertising.* London: Boyars.

Williamson, J. (1986). Woman is an island: Femininity and colonization. In T. Modleski (Ed.), *Studies in entertainment: Critical approaches to mass culture* (pp. 99–118). Bloomington: Indiana University Press.

MASS COMMUNICATION & SOCIETY, 2000, *3*(4), 439–452

SCHOLARLY MILESTONES ESSAY

Memoirs of a Commodity Fetishist

Stuart Ewen

Department of Film and Media Studies
Hunter College

The author, a central figure in the development of critical studies of advertising and consumer culture, discusses his intellectual influences and the issues raised by his work. He begins with his preacademic life, followed by a review of the genesis of his thinking about advertising and consumer culture as well as some key debates that emerged around his early book, Captains of Consciousness: Advertising and the Social Roots of the Consumer Culture. *The essay also addresses shifts in his thinking about media and in his creative work. The author argues for more attention to the issue of media literacy.*

Thirty-seven years ago, when I was a freshman history major at the University of Wisconsin, consumerism, the mass media, and the commercial culture more generally were not yet included within the liberal arts curricula of most colleges and universities. Although these institutions had been leaving tractor marks across the American social landscape for more than a century, few historians saw advertising, consumerism, or the apparatus of mass impression as subjects worthy of serious inquiry. Quite the contrary. For many in academia, ignorance about such matters was regarded as a litmus test of intelligence.[1]

This scholastic blind spot posed a problem for me. I was, after all, a child of post-World War II America, a time and place where economic prosperity and

---

Requests for reprints should be sent to Stuart Ewen, Department of Film and Media Studies, Hunter College, CUNY, 695 Park Avenue, New York, NY 10021. E-mail: drstu@bway.net

[1]Of the modern media of communication, only film—lifted to the status of an art form by French literati in *Cahiers du cinéma*—had begun to gain grudging acceptance within the official world of ideas.

dissected the ways that corporate capitalism infused every aspect of daily life, down to the language we speak, only invigorated this view. In my activities as a new left pamphleteer and in my ongoing study of history, these were the issues that shaped my intellectual development.

At the same time, however, there was something about Marcuse and the Frankfurt School that disturbed me. Despite their profound critique of American mass culture, there was a decidedly European and elitist quality to their writings. Whereas many of my history student friends in Wisconsin pursued advanced degrees in European intellectual history, seeking to connect to the world of Marcuse and his peers, I was committed to engaging the American experience more directly. As I began graduate school at the University of Rochester, American history and the history of American consumer culture became my passion.

Two teachers, very different in outlook, informed my work. One was Herbert Gutman, an avuncular social historian who, in his studies of working people in slavery and freedom, saw ordinary people as the authors of their own lives. Although he found my perspective on the ways that corporate ideology leavened the popular imagination to be misguided, his insistence that society is a battleground, not an iron cage, has stayed with me. Gutman also introduced me to E. P. Thompson's (1968/1991) "Time, Work-Discipline, and Industrial Capitalism," a brilliant essay that highlighted the extent to which 19th century capitalism, more than an economic system, encompassed a new perceptual universe that sought to eradicate earlier ways of seeing. This essay left a deep mark on me, and I continue to assign it to my own graduate students.

The other was Loren Baritz, whose interest in the history of American elites supported my research into the ideas of the men and women who pioneered in the creation of a 20th-century merchandising culture. Tips from Baritz led me to *Printers' Ink,* the advertising trade journal, and also to the writings of Edward Bernays as well as many other sources that still haunt the bibliographies of my writings.

Baritz encouraged me to reject many of the rules that shaped graduate studies in history at the time and, to a large extent, continue to. One was the 50-year rule, which advised historians against approaching subjects that were too contemporary. Another was the canon directing graduate students to write small doctoral dissertations, narrowly focused monographs that began with a review of existing literature and in the pages that followed made an original, if usually minor, contribution to the history of an already-existing field. Big books were for senior historians, people who had earned their stripes. A third injunction was against popularizing, writing for a general audience. Academic history, at its best, should be of interest primarily to other historians. Most important, Baritz was enthusiastic about my interest in studying the history of mass consumption and advertising, fields that did not yet exist. My approach, questioning the ruling faiths of American society and exploring advertising as an instrument of power, was connected to issues he had written about in his book *Servants of Power* (Bartiz, 1960).

For his research seminar in 1969, I wrote a paper entitled "Advertising as Social Production," which delved into the ways that a number of early 20th-century businessmen—forward-thinking capitalists like Edward Filene, along with architects of modern advertising—looked to *consumptionism,* as business strategist Christine Frederick termed it, as the salve that would tranquilize working class militancy while expanding the prosperity of business. This paper eventually became the first part of *Captains of Consciousness.*

Although many professors in the history department thought I was smart but loony—a perception fortified by my involvement in a guerrilla theater stunt wherein General Maxwell Taylor, of the Joint Chiefs, was presented with a pig's head—I was energized by the enthusiastic response of many fellow graduate students. The paper caused a stir for its novel subject matter and for its critical approach. Beyond Rochester, it was read, soon published, and then anthologized. I was 24, and with the help of my most influential teacher, Elizabeth Ewen, I was ready to write, not a dissertation as usually conceived but a book about a subject that, at least outside the academy, was of undeniable interest.

Doing research in the Widener Library and the Baker Business Library (both at Harvard), I felt like a spy, following a mass consumer culture, and the commercial propaganda machinery that propelled it, in the making. What blew me away, what still blows me away, was the extent to which the people I was uncovering, who never expected their words to be scrutinized except by their peers, were remarkably candid about their thoughts and intentions. As innovators, people formulating ideas and inventing practices that only in time would become routine, many were also exceptionally conscious of their moment in history and of their objectives in relation to that history. Writing from the vantage point of the early 1970s, where psychologically charged advertising was an unequivocal fact of life, one needed to look backward, to a period of origination, to better understand the present.

Oddly, given the ubiquity of its subject matter, *Captains of Consciousness: Advertising and the Social Roots of the Consumer Culture,* published in 1976, became the first scholarly history to critically evaluate advertising and consumer culture as defining forces in American life. In three sections, the book examined the roots of modern advertising in the early 20th century and explored the social, intellectual, and economic forces that propelled its development. Rather than looking at advertisements one by one, as individual attempts to sell a product or service, the book approached advertising overall as a widely iterated commentary on issues of want and desire, a new philosophical system, a pivotal medium by which a new, consumerist way of life was shaped, depicted, communicated, and sold.

It also looked at advertising as it embodied more expansive business goals, as a pivotal way that American corporations responded to, adjusted to, and exploited the social conditions, economic consequences, and new ways of seeing that emerged with the rise of a mass production system. Mass production required mass consumption, and I found that a growing number of businessmen were beginning to speak of the ways that human instinct needed to be mobilized to turn consumption into an inner compulsion. I also explored the extent to which mass consumption and advertising were seen as a business response to the perceived threat of socialism.

Advertising also provided a fascinating window through which one could see capitalism shifting from an economy defined primarily by production, as it was in the 19th century, to one that over the course of the 20th century would be increasingly defined by consumption. The virtual disappearance of the factory from corporate imagery and the conscious cultivation of emotional links between corporate goods and the personal lives of consumers provided a clairvoyant snapshot of the world to come. The book also posed questions about the ways that advertising helped to establish prevailing models of the self, the family, and the good life in American consumer society. The ways that advertising helped to alter customary notions of truth and public expression were also probed. Although research for the book was limited, for the most part, to the years between 1900 and 1930, its thesis, and my conscious intent, was to explore the dream life of the 20th century. Unlike much historical writing, *Captains* was audacious, impassioned, overtly political, and—in ways that implied where I would need to go in future research and writing—unfinished. It also quickly gathered an audience.

Attacked by editorials and articles in *Advertising Age,* the book was widely reviewed and became an academic best seller. Cutting across disciplines, it was adopted as a required text in classes ranging from history to sociology to communications and marketing. As people in the visual arts became increasingly conscious of and uneasy about advertising as the preeminent public art form, art and art history programs also assigned the book.

From the time it was published, *Captains of Consciousness* attracted both notice and controversy. It was praised in *Newsweek* and other prominent newspapers and magazines, but it was also widely denounced. It received a Best Business Book award from the *Library Journal,* which, only a few issues before, had savaged the book. It was named an Outstanding Academic Book by *Choice* magazine, although elsewhere its objectivity was questioned and its so-called Marxist disposition was often cited as grounds for immediate dismissal. Marshall McLuhan sent passages to Canadian Prime Minister Pierre Trudeau, but *The Birmingham News* reviewer declared that "the book is mostly junk."

Captains clearly resonated for many people. Although a book about history, it was recognizable, offering a look at some ideas and actions that had given rise to a world that they knew. I did not expect this book, written while I was in my 20s, to install me as a founder of the field, but I was not completely shocked by people's interest. In spite of inbred academic evasions, its subject was conspicuous, in need of a history. At a moment when the prevailing structures of American power were widely being questioned and sacred cows were on the dinner menu of a generation, its combative sensibility was also faithful to its time.

In staking out an academic subject matter of wide interest and offering a critical perspective about a subject that people tend to have strong feelings about, *Captains of Consciousness* had the salutary effect of countenancing a generation of young—and a few older—scholars to address the questions that it had opened. In universities and other public forums, advertising and the paradigms of consumer ideology were becoming central to the ways that American society was being interpreted and understood. Fortuitously, *Captains* was among the first books to bring these issues to the stage of intellectual life, something that has often made it an underpinning or a target for subsequent work.

In the late 1970s and early 1980s, a body of historical and sociological writing on advertising and consumer culture began to appear. Judith Williamson's (1978) book, *Decoding Advertisements*, published in England, used semiotics to explore the construction of meaning in contemporary advertising. *The Making of Modern Advertising*, by Daniel Pope (1983), offered a more detailed picture of the industry than I had drawn. An anthology, *The Culture of Consumption,* edited by Richard Fox and Jackson Lears (1983), appeared in the same year. Throughout the 1980s, the literature on advertising grew. Roland Marchand's (1985) *Advertising the American Dream,* an excellent book; Bill Leiss, Stephen Kline, and Sut Jhally's (1986) *Social Communication in Advertising;* and Michael Schudson's (1984) *Advertising, The Uneasy Persuasion* all appeared between 1984 and 1986. All cited *Captains,* but Schudson's was a rancorous counterattack. Arguing that *Captains* was "naive [and] without ... historical foundation," Schudson wrote a syrupy and myopic polemic on behalf of advertising and at the same time an argument that advertising has had little influence on American society. The public differences between us comprised one of the first academic debates over the role of advertising in American life.[2]

Less venomous than Schudson's in its assault, Lears's (Fox & Lear, 1983) opening essay in *The Culture of Consumption,* subtitled "Advertising and the Therapeutic Roots of the Consumer Culture," may have appropriated its cadence from the subtitle of *Captains, Advertising and the Social Roots of the Consumer Culture* but also took time to elevate itself above the erroneousness that I and historian Daniel Boorstin (1961), in his book *The Image,* brought to the subject of advertising:

---

[2]People interested in looking into the debate may wish to read Schudson's book, as well as my review, Ewen (1985a). A heated follow-up to the review appeared in the next issue, when Schudson sympathizer Ivan Preston denounced the journal for asking me to review the book. My response to Preston was included (see Ewen, 1985b). The debate was also the subject of Man Kong Lum's (1989) doctoral dissertation, *Captains and Corporals: A Critical Analysis of the Debate in the United States Between the Neo-Marxist and the Reflective Perspectives on Advertising.* There were some rather vehement personal correspondences surrounding my review, from Schudson and Preston to journal editor George Gerbner, which for now remain private.

The few historians who have addressed the subject in recent years tend to fall into two opposing camps, best represented by Daniel Boorstin and Stuart Ewen. Boorstin thoughtfully sketches some moral and emotional dilemmas in the culture of consumption, but he ignores power relations. ... Ewen, on the other hand, can see nothing but power relations. To him the consumer is the product of a conspiracy hatched by corporate executives in the bowels of the Ministry of Truth, then imposed with diabolical cleverness on a passive population. Neither Ewen nor Boorstin grasps the complex relationship between power relations and changes in values—between advertisers' changing strategies and the cultural confusion at the turn of the century.

When one looks beneath such protests, much of Lears's work on advertising has been an offshoot of my own, but his characterization of *Captains* as conspiracy theory, an accusation that has been reiterated by some others, merits a brief response. I am not one to assume that conspiracies have played no role in history or that propagandists have never been involved in them, but what I presented in *Captains of Consciousness* was not the story of a conspiracy. Rather, it was a review of business thinking during the time that mass production was taking hold and modern advertising was being developed, and it revealed the extent to which a broad number of business leaders were harboring similar thoughts. This is not conspiracy; it's the history of ideas. The book simply recorded the evolving consciousness of a number of American business people, in different quarters, during a period of social, economic, and strategic transition. That their conceits dovetailed is not because they plotted in some "ministry of truth." It only indicates that they faced common problems and, using available tools, were conceiving congruous responses to their world. The innovations of individuals seldom occur in a vacuum.

That their inventions were spontaneously "imposed on a passive population" was never my argument, and the overtly political disposition of my book and of my later writings assumes that the population is not only capable of resisting but must resist the miasma of commercialism when it threatens to inundate other ways of seeing and imagining. It also assumes that, at times, people are capable of being persuaded or seduced, even against their own best interests.

Captains of Consciousness was, without question, a spiritual child of the 1960s. The passion as well as the attacks it attracted cannot be divorced from the fervent feelings that are still inspired by that time. This intrinsic connection to arguments that continue to define American social, cultural, and political life may explain why it has remained of interest to readers. A new edition is currently in preparation. In an age where the shelf life of books is most often brief, this endurance is gratifying, but it is also a testament to the fact that its subject matter has become an increasingly pervasive and, for many, problematic element of life.

Although my interest in commercial culture and in the dynamics of power perseveres, I've undergone a number of intellectual changes since *Captains* first appeared. In terms of research and writing, I've become more and more interested in the question of visual eloquence, the ways that images—even in silence—converse with people and vice versa. *Channels of Desire* (1982/1992), a book of essays written with my running mate Liz Ewen, took us beyond advertising into people's encounters with a range of visual media (e.g., movies, fashion, even labels on cans of evaporated milk) to understand better the social and psychological meaning of consumption. *All Consuming Images* (1988/1999) investigated architecture, corporate logos, industrial design, product packaging, and body ideals as historical focal points, places where complex issues of social power in different ways and in different times take on the apparent simplicity of beauty. In *PR! A Social History of Spin* (1996), I revisited some concerns addressed in my first book, focusing on the rise of public relations, which is closely connected to advertising.

Some of what I learned researching *PR!* would have made *Captains of Consciousness* a more complete and, perhaps to its detriment, much longer book. My readings into the rise of social psychology, commencing with Gustave LeBon's *The Crowd* (1896), would have provided me with a more penetrating picture of what advertising people of the 1920s meant when they spoke of their desire to organize the instincts. Research into the Committee on Public Information, the propaganda bureau established during the First World War, would have explained how a national persuasion industry was jump-started and why advertising specialists of the 1920s were so at ease with the idea of molding other people's minds. My investigation of the American Way campaign by the National Association of Manufacturers or of the 1939 World's Fair would have added strength and depth to my section on the political ideology of consumption.

Since the mid-1970s, when *Captains* was published, the global reach of American commercial culture has only accelerated. In the 1980s, commercialism mushroomed into a vehement global religion. Where advertising once inhabited circumscribed arenas—television, radio, newspapers, magazines, billboards—today nearly every moment of human attention is converted into an occasion for a sales pitch, while notions of the public interest and noncommercial arenas of expression are under assault.

In the wake of these developments, it is encouraging that a growing number of people, crossing disciplines, are making various aspects of media and popular culture the subject matter of study. Although much in the fields of media and cultural studies fails to address the dynamics of corporate power in the modern world, students today are more likely than in the past to learn about the social history of the mass media and the elements of cultural experience, commercial and otherwise, that mark life at the onset of the 21st century. Within such inquiries, issues such as the consolidation of media ownership, the powerful role of perception management in today's society, and the steady commercialization of nearly every human experience will, by force of circumstance, increasingly come to the fore.

These developments, corresponding with my experiences as a teacher, have had a deep effect on how I think about the work I do and about the issues and politics of culture. If, in the 1970s, the critical exegesis of consumer society seemed an appropriate response to the world, from the early 1980s onward I've become increasingly concerned with the pivotal importance of reinvigorating the public sphere, moving beyond the boosterism of a business-driven culture and deepening the possibility of meaningful public discussion.

I am convinced that for us, and for our students, the critical study of media and society needs to be integrated with strategies for enriching and broadening the quality of public expression. In many ways this fusion is a descendent of objectives that have been central to the rise of democratic movements over the past few centuries, those of universal literacy and public education.

Historically, links between literacy and democracy are inseparable from the notion of an informed populace, conversant with the issues that touch upon their lives, enabled with tools that allow them to participate actively in public deliberation and social change. Nineteenth-century struggles for literacy and education were never limited to the ability to read. They were also about learning to write and thus about expanding the number and variety of voices heard in published interchanges and debates. Literacy was about crossing the lines that had historically separated men of ideas from ordinary people, about the social enfranchisement of those who been excluded from the compensations of citizenship.

This is palpable in the life of Frederick Douglass (1855), who repeatedly recounted an incident from his childhood in which the mistress of the plantation where he was a slave carelessly began teaching him to read. When discovered, she was severely reprimanded by her husband. She had, as Douglass explained it, violated "the true philosophy of slavery, and the peculiar rules necessary to be observed by masters and mistresses, in the management of their human chattels." From this episode a "painful mystery" was unraveled for Douglass. It explained to him the way that enforced illiteracy buttressed "the white man's power to perpetuate the enslavement of the black man." Douglass took this lesson and, running away from slavery to the North, became not only a reader but more important a writer, the leading Black abolitionist. The written word was the primary tool of public knowledge, and in the 19th century literacy was essential as the voices of African Americans became part of the antislavery debate.

Today these issues remain, yet the terrain of literacy has significantly changed. Those of us engaged in media education need to take the lead in rethinking and regenerating the demand for universal literacy. In the final chapter of *PR!*, "The Public and Its Problems: Some Notes for the New Millennium," I addressed this concern directly.

> In a society where instrumental images are employed to petition our affections at every turn—often without a word—educational curricula must...encourage the development of tools for critically analyzing images. Going back some time, the language of images has been well known to people working in the field of opinion management.

For democracy to prevail, image making as a communicative activity must be understood by ordinary citizens as well. The aesthetic realm—and the enigmatic ties linking aesthetic, social, economic, political, and ethical values—must be brought down to earth as a subject of study.

The development of curricula in media and visual literacy will not only sharpen people's ability to decipher their world, but it will also contribute to a broadening of the public sphere. Literacy is never just about reading; it is also about writing. Just as early campaigns for universal print literacy were concerned with democratizing the tools of public expression—the written word—upcoming struggles for media literacy must strive to empower people with contemporary implements of public discourse: video, graphic arts, photography, computer-assisted journalism and layout, and performance. More customary mainstays of public expression—expository writing and public speaking—must be resuscitated as well.

Media literacy cannot simply be seen as a vaccination against PR or other familiar strains of institutionalized guile. It must be understood in an education in techniques that can democratize the realm of public expression and will magnify the possibility of meaningful public interactions. Distinctions between publicist and citizen, author and audience, need to be broken down. Education can facilitate this process. It can enlarge the circle of who is permitted—and who will be able—to interpret and make sense of the world. (pp. 413–414)

Practically, such concerns have become central to my creative work and my teaching over the past 20 years. As a kid, and into my 20s, I passed a good deal of time making pictures. It was something we did in my family. In the mid-1960s, my belief in the need to work and experiment with visual form affected the look and feel of the underground newspaper *Connections*. As I pursued and completed my graduate work, however, and in my early years of teaching, I put this part of me aside, focusing on critical writing and research and preparing new courses.

By the early 1980s, however, I felt compelled to return to a more multimedia approach to expression. Partly it was therapeutic. I found, and find, image making and the creative blending of word and image more pleasurable than the austere activity of writing. The shift was also a result of my first decade of teaching, when I observed the ways that critical analysis, in the absence of alternative media making, often left students feeling cynical and voiceless.

On a personal level, I dreamed up an alter ego, Archie Bishop, whose work as a graphic artist, photographer, pamphleteer, multimedia prankster, and political situationist has occupied a good part of my life since 1980. It began with an individual political art project called *Billboards of the Future,* weekly photocopied flyers handed out on the street, posted on walls, and distributed by mail, offering visual commentary on the mental and political afflictions of Reaganism (for some particulars, see Ewen, 1986).

My penchant for visual recreation carried over to book writing as well. Starting with *All Consuming Images,* my books have included a number of Archie's visual pieces, although within their pages I never acknowledged the extent to which he and I were related. A current book project that I'm working on with Liz Ewen—a three century panorama exploring the bizarre history of stereotyping, to be called *Type-Casting: On the Arts & Sciences of Human Inequality*—will be even more visual in nature.

In the mid-1990s, *Billboards of the Future* became more collective, and together with students and assorted friends I began organizing large-scale street installations, about one a year, beginning with "Gravestones for Democracy" in 1995. That exhibit occupied a city block in Manhattan and provided a spooky visual springboard for a month and a half of demonstrations against budget cuts that were hitting the City University of New York (CUNY), where I teach. Along the way I've acquired computer graphics know-how and recently made a short digital film, a comedy probing the ambiguous relations between media and reality called "'Live Feed' Live."

These intellectual and creative ventures have been mirrored in my undergraduate and graduate teaching as well. In my analytical undergraduate courses at Hunter College, I routinely ask students to produce work that is designed to hone their ability to communicate ideas in a variety of media. I also teach an advanced graphics workshop, where students are given problems to solve using a mix of visual, written, and exhibition skills to explore issues and ideas eloquently and publicly.

Working with doctoral students at the CUNY Graduate Center, I expect students to think about writing for a general public and have required that they create a magazine at the end of the class, using written work for the course but combining it with visual materials and creative layout. An example of Cult.Shock, the most recent incarnation of my graduate students' magazine project, which has recently become an online publication, is found at: http://www.cultshock.org.

In the Department of Film and Media Studies (formerly Communications) at Hunter College, this trajectory has been nourished by contact with students and colleagues and by the evolution of our undergraduate and graduate programs. When I first came to Hunter in 1977, the media studies curriculum offered mostly analytical courses, investigating the role of the media in history and in contemporary society.[3] Since the mid-1980s, this has changed dramatically. Alongside strong analytical courses, there has been a growing commitment to providing students with workshop courses in the modern tools of expression, designed to encourage them to explore new ways of seeing, speaking, and circulating their work. To reinforce this commitment, we've brought innovative alternative media makers onto the faculty, people who—while continuing their creative work—are committed to providing an unusually diverse, mostly working-class student body with a better ability to have a say in a society where media know-how is essential to being heard. Combining crit-

---

[3]Two print journalism courses taught by James Aronson, cofounder of *The National Guardian*, were the among the few exceptions to this predominantly academic orientation.

ical analysis with innovative course work in film, video, print, and interactive media, we have built one of the most interesting undergraduate programs in the country and have become, faculty and students alike, a fertile creative community.

We are now in the process of launching a Master of Fine Arts Program (MFA) in Integrated Media Arts, which will offer advanced studies in nonfiction media making, informed by a strong analytical foundation.[4] To me, these institutional developments are not simply the sum of my job. They are an outer expression of concerns that have evolved over a period of more than 3 decades.

Although the preceding narrative has taken the form of an abbreviated intellectual autobiography, it cannot be understood as simply a personal story. The issues and activities I've pursued have corresponded to more and more people moving toward the study and practice of media. From the publication of Daniel Boorstin's (1961) book, *The Image: A Guide to Pseudo-Events in America*, Marshall McLuhan's (1964) *Understanding Media*, and Herbert Schiller's (1969) *Mass Communications and American Empire,* there began to be a growing awareness that the history and impact of mass-mediated culture was altering the physics of power and perception on a global scale. I was part of the first generation of students who felt an urgency around the need to face the media question.

Our intellectual and creative choices reflected the social facts of the second half of the 20th century and the fateful challenges posed for those who, in a world where more and more people are touched by the media yet fewer and fewer control the pipelines of persuasion, ponder the fate of democracy. That the issues of advertising and consumer culture, along with the politics and economics of modern media systems, have become so paramount as subjects of study is an unavoidable consequence of our time. How we continue to respond to these issues, critically and through social action, provides a compelling agenda for the future.

REFERENCES

Baritz, L. (1960). *The servants of power: A history of the use of social science in American history.* Middletown, CT: Wesleyan Unveristy Press.
Boorstin, D. (1961). *The image: Or, what happened to the American dream.* New York: Atheneum.
Douglass, F. (1855). *My bondage and my freedom.* New York: Miller, Orton, & Mulligan.

---

[4]Beyond analytical seminars and an interdisciplinary research requirement, Master of Fine Arts Program (MFA) students must complete six workshops in three comprehensive areas, entitled Words, Visions, and Channels. The first will include courses in which journalism, script and treatment writing, and other forms of nonfiction media writing are a primary concern. The second will include courses where the visual communication of stories, ideas, and information serves as an overarching consideration. The third embraces courses where designs for distributing and exhibiting media work, for publicizing ideas, and for using media to enhance the quality of community interaction are dominant. The objective of the program is to educate socially aware media practitioners, capable in a wide range of media skills.

Ewen, S. (1976). *Captains of consciousness: Advertising and the social roots of the consumer culture.* New York: McGraw-Hill.

Ewen, S. (1985a). Colloquy. *Journal of Communication, 35,* 192–196.

Ewen, S. (1985b). Colloquy on book review ethics. *Journal of Communication, 35,* 224.

Ewen, S. (1986). A short history of billboards of the future. In J. Becker, G. Hedebro, & L. Paldán (Eds.), *Communication and domination: Essays to honor Herbert I. Schiller* (pp. 249–258). Norwood, NJ: Ablex.

Ewen, S. (1996). *PR! A social history of spin.* New York: Basic.

Ewen, S. (1999). *All consuming images: The politics of style in contemporary culture* (Rev. ed.). New York: Basic.

Ewen, S., & Ewen, E. (1992). *Channels of desire: Mass images and the making of American conciousness* (Rev. ed.). Minneapolis: University of Minnesota Press.

Fox, R. W., & Jackson Lears, T. J. (Eds.). (1983). *The culture of consumption: Critical essays in American history 1880–1980.* New York: Pantheon.

LeBon, G. (1896). *The crowd: A study of the popular mind.* London: Unwin.

Leiss, W., Kline, S., Jhally, S. (1986). *Social communication in advertising: Persons, products, & images of well-being.* New York: Methuen.

Lum, M. K. (1989). *Captains and corporals: A critical analysis of the debate in the United States between the neo-Marxist and the reflective perspectives on advertising.* Unpublished doctoral dissertation, New York University.

Marchand, R. (1985). *Advertising the American dream: Making way for modernity, 1920–1940.* Berkeley: University of California Press.

Marcuse, H. (1964). *One dimensional man; studies in the ideology of advanced industrial society.* Boston: Beacon.

McLuhan, M. (1964). *Understanding media: The extensions of man.* New York: McGraw-Hill.

Pope, D. (1983). *The making of modern advertising.* New York: Basic.

Schiller, H. L. (1969). *Mass communications and American empire.* New York: Kelley.

Schudson, M. (1984). *Advertising, the uneasy persuasion: Its dubious impact on American society.* New York: Basic.

Thompson, E. P. (1991). *Time, work discipline and industrial capitalism.* London: Merlin. (Original work published 1968)

Williamson, J. (1978). *Decoding advertisements: Ideology and meaning in advertising.* London: Boyars.

MASS COMMUNICATION & SOCIETY, 2000, 3(4), 453–456

BOOK REVIEWS

Jeffery A. Smith. *War and Press Freedom: The Problem of Prerogative Power*, New York: Oxford University Press, 1999, 324 pp., ISBN No. 0–19–509945–1 (cloth), ISBN No. 0–19–509946–X (paper).

Reviewed by Paul McMasters
First Amendment Ombudsman, The Freedom Forum
Arlington, Virginia

On the front lines, the right information in the wrong hands can be as deadly as bullets or bombs. Military officers recognize that the careful management of information is essential to the safety of their troops and the success of their missions. As that battlefield imperative has moved up the ranks toward the office of the commander in chief, however, too often it has been transformed into a rationale for censoring the press and the public for uttering not only information but ideas and opinions as well. Jeffery A. Smith has set out to document how that process, dressed up in the doctrine of executive prerogative, flouts both the U.S. Constitution and democratic principles. The result is a book of consequence about issues of moment.

Of all the powers distributed by the U.S. Constitution, perhaps the most awesome is the declaration of war. The Constitution places that power with Congress. During the 2 centuries of the existence of this nation, however, Congress has declared war only five times, yet presidents have sent American troops abroad more than 200 times (p. 193).

That history raises questions going to our constitutional core. By what authority does the president assert the power to make war? Does that extraconstitutional power include the authority to abridge freedom of the press? How relevant is the Constitution to the life of a democracy if it can be suspended so effortlessly in times of crisis, when the rule of law seems to be most important?

Smith's historical perspective is that the Constitution was drafted in crisis to serve in crisis. As Chief Justice Charles Evans Hughes (*Home Building and Loan Association v. Blaisdall,* 1934) wrote: "Its grants of power to the Federal Government and its limitations of the power of the States were determined in the light of emergency and they are not altered by emergency." Unfortunately, censorship during wartime is routine and accepted, accomplished by the same sort of royal prerog-

BOOK REVIEWS

ative exercised by the Tudor and Stuart monarchs that the framers had expressly sought to deny the president of the United States.

Yet almost from the birth of the nation, during times of war and military crisis, the executive prerogative has been invoked. Presidents and generals have imposed censorship on journalists, federal and state officials, dissidents, and ordinary citizens. Some were detained or arrested; some spent years in prisons. Newspaper offices were sacked and burned. The federal government took over railroad, telegraph, cable, and postal operations for purposes of controlling the flow of information. Secret plans were drawn for shadowy agencies under orders to suspend the Constitution and impose martial law when the call from the White House came.

All this took place with the cooperation or acquiescence of Congress, the courts, the public, and, yes, many journalists and news executives. The Constitution aside, more than 470 laws were passed to install the machinery of mandatory and voluntary censorship. Dozens of dubious Supreme Court decisions validated those laws, under which journalists were denied information and punished for what they obtained on their own. Thousands of dissidents and members of certain nationalities were imprisoned, as were journalists, legislators, and a judge or two.

The engine of this sad litany was primarily the executive prerogative. That prerogative owes its legal substance to the notion that there is a higher law than the Constitution. That principle is "older than the written constitution," according to Garrard Glenn (*The Army and the Law*, 1918); "the rights of the individual must yield to those of the State in the time of the State's peril from the public enemy." Under the presidential prerogative, the chief executive may invoke this law of self-preservation when threats to national security rise. Smith challenges the rationale as well as the constitutionality of that power. Even if it were valid, he contends, it should not extend to freedom of the press.

In the three chapters of Part One of *War and Press Freedom*, Smith marshals a formidable knowledge of the origins of the Constitution to make the case that the press clause of the First Amendment is not subject to rescission by either the legislative or executive branch, even in wartime. The detail and documentation he presents are persuasive. Part Two, consisting of four chapters, is a relentless recitation of the actual uses of presidential prerogative and other executive powers in curtailing the press. Part Three, a single chapter, presents more detail on how badly the press was treated at the hands of the military and the White House; it also shows how some members of the press were complicit in denying information to their colleagues and the public. In a final chapter, Smith concludes that the press and the military need one another and that their unique functions serve democracy. He wrote, "In theory press freedom can cost lives, but in reality the incompetence and unsound policies journalists should be exposing are the most serious hazards in the domain of national security" (p. 227).

This book elaborates on and expands ideas Smith presented in an article appearing in the Spring 1987 issue of *William & Mary Law Review*. It benefits greatly from exhaustive research and seems rather naturally to build on his two previous books, *Printers and Press Freedom: The Ideology of Early American Idealism* (1988) and *Franklin and Bache: Envisioning the Enlightened Republic* (1990). Smith's new book appears about the same time as two others with related themes, although they are narrower in scope: *Free Speech in the Good War: Defining an American Ideal, 1939–1945* by Richard Steele (1999) and *Terrorism & The Constitution: Sacrificing Civil Liberties in the Name of National Security* by James X. Dempsey and David Cole (1999).

In his effort to cover so much ground, Smith scants some history, some constitutional doctrine, and some court cases. That and an occasional organizational tic aside, Smith's scholarship, writing ability, and an impressive array of resources produce an enormously informing work. Each page peels back another layer of what Smith calls "autocratic lawlessness." The cumulative impact is a display of the durability of the idea that the "parchment barrier" of the Constitution is no match for the panic provoked by wars and rumors of wars. It is troubling to be reminded how frequently the stampede to rally round the flag has trampled the Constitution in the dirt.

This book tarnishes some heroes. A succession of civil liberties champions—with the notable exception of James Madison—seem to have lost their First Amendment compass once in the White House. Abraham Lincoln is one of them. As much as any other president, it seems, he legitimized the idea of executive prerogative. Lincoln asked, "Must a government of necessity be too strong for the liberties of its people, or too weak to maintain its own existence?" The question presents a false choice, of course, because it assumes that freedom and survival are exclusive. The Civil War era presented unique challenges, more extreme in many aspects than other wars. Nevertheless, the actions of Lincoln and his subordinates under the executive prerogative validated what had gone before and sanctioned what was yet to come.

Public distrust is the inevitable product of such censorship. Those who impose it inevitably leave a shameful mark in the history books. Yet, nearly every president and military leader has to learn this bitter lesson with each new military crisis, as do journalists, judges, and ordinary citizens. Even though we emerged from the Cold War with a more supportive view of First Amendment freedoms during wartime, Smith points out that the damage had been done: "More court precedents had accumulated on the side of a misguided national security mentality that recognized a power for Congress to make laws abridging freedom of the press" (p. 65).

Throughout the book, Smith returns often to the idea that wartime restrictions on the press are an ironic affront to an institution that from its inception in this country focused on wars. Newspapers and journals of the colonial era were filled with news about wars, arguments about wars, and criticism of the kings who caused the deaths and suffering of their subjects to wage wars. This was a staple of the journalism the framers sought to protect in the First Amendment.

Overall, *War and Press Freedom* is a successful indictment of the executive prerogative wielded to restrict freedom of the press. The self-preservation argument loses its force when one considers that a nation that sacrifices freedom of the press and the right to speak freely to save itself is something less than it was before, if not actually something different. At any rate, the executive prerogative encourages democratic brinkmanship that a nation indulges at its peril. Perhaps an analogy would be to the man who leaps off a cliff to escape a purported enemy: The risk is not just that he may suffer terrible injuries but that he may form a dangerous habit.

REFERENCES

Dempsey, J. X., & Cole, D. (1999). *Terrorism & the Constitution: Sacrificing civil liberties in the name of national security.* Los Angeles: First Amendment Foundation.

Glenn, G. (1918). *The army and the law.* New York: Columbia University Press.

Home Building and Loan Association v. Blaisdell, 290 U.S. 398, 425 (1934).

Smith, J. A. (1988). *Printers and press freedom: The ideology of early American idealism.* New York: Oxford University Press.

Smith, J. A. (1990). *Franklin and Bache: Envisioning the enlightened republic.* New York: Oxford University Press.

Steele, R. W. (1999). *Free speech in the good war: Defining an American ideal, 1939–1945.* New York: St. Martins.